MATTHEW ROBBINS' *inspired* WEDDINGS

Designing Your Big Day with Favorite Objects & Family Treasures

Foreword MARTHA STEWART
Photographs THUSS+FARRELL

STEWART, TABORI & CHANG · NEW YORK

Published in 2011
by Stewart, Tabori & Chang
An imprint of ABRAMS

Content copyright © 2011 Matthew Robbins Design
Photographs copyright © 2011 THUSSFARRELL, LLC

Library of Congress Cataloging-in-Publication Data

Robbins, Matthew.
  Matthew Robbins' inspired weddings : designing your big day
with favorite objects and family treasures / by Matthew Robbins ;
foreword by Martha Stewart.
    p. cm.
  ISBN 978-1-58479-893-4
1. Weddings—Planning. I. Title. II. Title: Inspired weddings.
  HQ745.R625 2012
  395.2'2—dc22
                        2011008519

EDITOR: Jennifer Levesque
DESIGN: THUSS+FARRELL
PRODUCTION MANAGER: Ankur Ghosh

The text of this book was composed in HFJ Archer, Gotham, and
Mercury families.

Printed and bound in China
10 9 8 7 6 5 4 3 2 1

Stewart, Tabori & Chang books are available at special discounts
when purchased in quantity for premiums and promotions as well as
fundraising or educational use. Special editions can also be created to
specification. For details, contact specialsales@abramsbooks.com
or the address below.

THE ART OF BOOKS SINCE 1949

115 West 18th Street
New York, NY 10011
www.abramsbooks.com

for **JACK**

CONTENTS

FOREWORD

We have been working with the incredible Matthew Robbins for several years. His broad range of inspired ideas and his ability to design and create a wide assortment of vignettes or entire themes for weddings and parties from the humblest of materials to the most elaborate and lavish ingredients, never ceases to amaze and delight us.

This book, Matthew's first, is a charming how-to primer for those of us who desire to "make it ourselves."

Matthew is a collector, and he instills in us the ability to find and identify and round up those treasures that will be the basis for a theme. He shows us how a charming table can be set, how flowers can transform the ordinary into the extraordinary. He demonstrates the importance of color and color schemes in the planning process, Matthew is one of us, as evidenced in his choice of themes—citrus, seashells, French candy. Each theme focuses on a color palette, on objects that are "hunted and gathered," and on decorative details that are beautifully made and conceived.

Matthew is generous with his sources and points the reader to places where interesting "ingredients" can be found. It is these finds that make Matthew's events the special, personal, unique parties they are.

Thank you, Matthew, for your lovely book, wonderful ideas, and fine combinations of old and new.

Martha Stewart

INTRODUCTION

If you're like me, you love perusing the latest art and decorating books and magazines. I've always had a passion for art and good design, and I believe that we should surround ourselves with beauty to stay inspired and refreshed. In my career, I've brought this philosophy to every event and wedding I've had the pleasure of designing. I approach each party as an artist and I aim to create a beautiful world that reflects my client's personal style.

My career as an event designer began during my early college years as an art student. I was studying painting, printmaking, and art history in San Francisco, and I needed a part-time job on the weekends. I walked by a beautiful shop one afternoon on Market Street and instantly fell in love with the flowers, branches, and objects in the window. After giving it some thought, I decided to inquire about a job—and by the following week, I was working in my first flower shop! In just a few months' time, I found myself designing pieces for all of the shop's big accounts, and it had become quite clear that I had a passion for flowers. This job resulted in my meeting Maria Vella, now my dear friend and mentor. She quickly inspired in me a whole new level of curiosity and excitement for designing beautiful events. I became a sponge around her, absorbing everything there was to know about creating unique and inspired parties. Maria brings a lovely, effortless quality to her work and approach to life, which immediately influenced me, as it mirrored my own instinct to design with an eye for elegance and unfussy details.

After finishing college in California, I decided to make the big move to the East Coast. I was naïve but confident in my talents—so I thought, Why not tackle New York? After getting to know the industry in the big city, I started my own event décor company, which soon blossomed into what is now an amazing and accomplished business. I owe much of my success to Martha Stewart and her fantastic team, as they discovered and promoted my work from the moment it was out there. Within the first year of running my company, I was on *The Martha Stewart Show* on television and my work was on the cover of *Martha Stewart Weddings* magazine. I have now enjoyed ten years as a contributing editor to *Martha Stewart Weddings*. I will forever be grateful for Martha's knowledge of,

passion for, and commitment to good design. Over these ten years, I have also had amazing opportunities to work with the best of the best in the wedding, events, and design industries. Each new client or event brings fresh inspiration, which is ultimately why I adore what I do!

The Largest Dinner Party You've Ever Thrown

I like to encourage couples to think of their wedding as the largest dinner party they've ever thrown. Why? Because your wedding should fit in with the rest of your tastes and your lifestyle—it should not be the exception. You want to treat your guests as if you're welcoming them into your own home. Your wedding should look and feel like it's yours and nobody else's. Everything—from the invitations to the ceremony and the space itself—should be infused with personalized details that create an event unique to you.

If your goal is to plan a wedding that doesn't look like your friends' weddings and a million other weddings you've attended over the years, then this book is for you. You'll see how easy it is to take the things that you already love and use them to plan an event that is uniquely your own.

Be Your Own Most Important Client

My favorite part of designing and event planning is collaborating with my clients. Step one is getting to know the couple: I ask about what they like, what they read, what they wear, as well as what their favorite flowers, colors, and places to travel are, and even which restaurants they love. I also talk with them about whether they prefer a cleaner, more modern look, or one that's more rustic, or possibly even one that's ornate and traditional.

You should begin your process by asking yourself these same questions. This book will show you how. You won't find the latest trends, but rather an approach that will help make your wedding really feel like "you."

And what better way to start than with something that's already personal to you? You may not know what you want your wedding to *look* like, but you probably know exactly what you want it to *feel* like. For example, perhaps you want it to remind you of the classical blue and white of a Wedgwood heirloom that your grandmother gave you. Or maybe you want your big day to reflect a sense of who you and your partner are when you're together. Either way, a family heirloom or a small memento that you picked up on a romantic getaway can serve as the cornerstone and point of inspiration for your entire event.

This book shows you how any object can be used as the inspiration for your wedding décor. In the following chapters, I illustrate how nine very different, very personal objects can serve as the seeds for many unique and very personal wedding designs, from ceremony to reception, and all of the details in between. Along the way, you'll learn how to develop the special objects in your life into the wedding you've always wanted, but may not be able to imagine right now, regardless of your budget.

Hunting and Gathering for Your Wedding Inspiration

Think of planning your wedding as a process of hunting and gathering: You're hunting for personal, meaningful items and gathering design details that will allow you to bring out the elements you most love about these items. That's how I see my job. As a designer, I'm continually searching for new and unique inspiration. Fresh ideas can come from anywhere, be it an interesting trinket I pick up in a Paris flea market, or a beautiful piece of fruit at my local farmers' market. The key is to always keep your eyes open—you never know where you'll spot that little something that inspires your entire event!

What You'll Need for the Hunt

I keep the following things with me at all times when I'm planning an event, and you should too. These tools make the process easier by helping you to keep all of your inspirations in one place. You'll need:

- A sketchbook/notebook for keeping notes about the things you like and storing magazine tear sheets.
- A digital camera. Don't forget to take pictures of objects you love and the venues you visit.
- A great bag for gathering materials.

Six Steps for Successful Gathering

Here is my process for turning an inspiring object into your ideal wedding or event.

1. PREPARE. First things first, be open-minded as you create a list of shops and markets to scour for inspiring items. Sometimes the most beautiful objects can come from the most unexpected places.

2. HUNT. Look around and keep your eyes wide open! Travel, go shopping, go flea-marketing, and look through your closets too. And don't worry if the things that begin to inspire you don't take a cohesive shape at first; there will be time to edit later.

3. CONSIDER. Once you've chosen your inspirational object, begin by breaking down the elements of that object according to color, pattern, texture, material, shape, and the mood it evokes.

4. MAP. Next, envision how you want your event to unfold, and consider how your inspiration can enhance your chosen venue. Take some time to think about all of the logistical elements that you'll need to work out and determine how your inspiration might influence those as well.

5. MATCH. For me, this is the really fun part: Get creative and consider how and where you can incorporate your inspiration into all of the different aspects of your event. Think about all of the ways you can inject the color palette and mood into your affair.

6. GATHER. Now it's time for all of your inspired ideas to come to life. Once you've identified how to integrate your inspiration, go shopping, visit with your caterer, check out what your rental company has to offer, choose your invitations, stroll through the flower market, and start putting together your own truly inspired event!

GREAT PLACES TO GO HUNTING

One great place to hunt is your friends' houses, especially those whose style you admire. Use your loved ones as a resource and shop their shelves and collections. Now is the perfect time to see if you can borrow that keepsake from your friend's trip to Italy that you've always had your eye on. And, most important, take your stylish friends shopping with you!

- Flea markets
- Antique shops and dealers
- "Junk" shops
- Your grandmother's attic
- Your parents' basement
- Gourmet food shops—check out the beautifully designed imported packaging.
- Farmers' markets—they're great places to find homemade goods and produce.
- Art galleries and museums—maybe you'll leave with a postcard image of your favorite piece of artwork for inspiration.
- Fabric stores
- Knitting and quilting stores
- Notions stores—for buttons and trimmings
- Vintage-clothing stores
- Fashion, art, and decorating magazines
- Tile stores
- Plant and landscaping stores—these are great places to hunt for rich textures and vibrant colors.
- Local botanical gardens—flowers and plants can be so inspiring!
- High-end furniture stores
- Used bookstores—look for old interior design and art books, vintage postcards, and maps to get you going.
- Stationery and paper goods shops
- Candy stores—the fun packaging can serve as a great inspiration.
- Head to Chinatown and other ethnic neighborhoods near where you live for fun items that you don't see everywhere
- Visit local artisans and craftsmen while traveling—local woodworkers in Scandinavia, fabric artisans in India, and glassblowers in Venice are just a few examples.

CITRUS

Why Citrus?

I've always been drawn to fruits growing right on the branch. During my early professional years in Sonoma, I found myself obsessing over ripening nectarines. The transition that trees make from blossoms, to leaves, and then suddenly becoming heavy with fruit—the whole process—still fascinates me. Though I think all fruits maturing on the branch are beautiful, citrus fruits hold a special place in my heart; you can't grow up in Florida without loving them at least a little. Though my childhood laid the groundwork, it was really the several years I spent in sunny California that solidified my feelings for these juicy fruits.

What About the Palette?

Citrus fruits have so many wonderful qualities to draw from; everything about them inspires me. Of course their colors come to mind first; I love how strong and intense all the various hues are. The soft, round shape of a citrus fruit is particularly lovely; there are endless ways to incorporate that shape into an event, especially with your table setting. And don't forget about the flavors! There are countless ways to feature them, especially in your menu.

The bright yellow lemon, the sweet pink grapefruit, and the bold orange make for an amazing palette from which to design an event. You might be surprised to hear that my favorite part about the citrus palette, however, is actually the green of the leaves. I adore how crisp the green looks when paired with yellow and orange.

Who Is the Client?

I definitely envision a couple that dreams of a destination wedding; Perhaps Napa, Italy, or even the South of France calls to them. This couple is far from fussy, and is clearly interested in creating a comfortable yet amazingly beautiful environment for their guests to enjoy.

Where and When?

What's wonderful about this palette is its seasonal range. You'll find it easy to feature these tones from spring through summer and all the way into fall, making them a versatile choice. The whole inspiration feels perfect for a wedding set in a vineyard, overlooking a gorgeous, sprawling vista. The juicy orange, yellow, and white color palette is bright, airy, and crisp, making it most ideal for a warm summer day or evening.

My Focus

My focus in this chapter is to create a feeling of effortless abundance—very easy, friendly, and totally approachable.

MOOD •
Citrus fruits conjure up warm
thoughts of summer evenings
spent sipping wine in Napa
Valley, California.

SHAPE/FORM •
The soft, round shape of these
fruits is truly lovely; there are
endless ways to incorporate
this feature into your event.

COLORS •
I adore how crisp the green
of the leaves looks when
paired with warm yellow- and
orange-toned citrus fruits.

HUNTED AND GATHERED

OPPOSITE I find the perfectly round shape of citrus fruits appealing, so I used that as a guide when picking out many of these pieces. The other driving force, besides the palette, of course, is that beautiful juicy moment when you first slice open an orange; I tried to reflect that in the shiny surfaces of most of these objects. For me, this whole inspiration is about yummy, juicy, delicious objects.

BIG ROUND ORANGE PLACEMAT—I like the idea of using a round placemat in lieu of a charger plate for a more casual affair.

ROUND WOODEN BOWL—The wood tones are such a beautiful accent to this bright and cheery palette.

FELT—These little round felt coasters are easy to make on your own and are quite cute.

ORANGE CAPIZ SHELL BOWL—The slightly reflective nature of the capiz shell reminds me of the glistening inside of freshly cut citrus fruits.

SMALL WOVEN TRAY—The size of this little tray is what drew me in.

LITTLE CHERRIES—Okay sure, cherries are not citrus fruits, but the color mimics that of a fresh blood orange, making it a great little accent.

ORANGE MARMALADE—Yum!

DECORATIVE RIBBON—The design on this Bell'occhio ribbon is really special; the fruits and birds are so charming.

VINTAGE ORANGE VASE—I love the shape of this vase, and the color couldn't be more spot-on.

GREEN GLASS VASE—The green glaze on this glass vase is quite beautiful against all of this orange.

TINY GLASS PITCHER—The coloring of this little pitcher reminds me of orange cream soda.

BELOW, OPPOSITE This table setting is a more modern interpretation of our citrus inspiration. The bright, cheery palette still shines, but the whole vibe is a bit more clean and chic. I went on the hunt for some vessels that captured the particular, slightly squat roundness of the citrus fruit. The openings to these glazed ceramic vessels weren't all that large, but in this case it didn't matter, as I filled them with these huge, show-stopping peonies in a bright, lemony yellow. Since each bloom was so lavish and open, I only needed four or five to make a big impact. I tucked in a few kumquats for a little added whimsy. To play up the juiciness of the citrus, I used these pretty glazed plates in an orange hue. I love white and orange together—it's such a delicious, summery palette that feels very Italian—so I topped each plate with a crisp white napkin, and brought the centerpiece down into each setting by placing a sprig of kumquat atop the linens. To finish things off, I brought in some shiny silver flatware and these graceful wineglasses, which bring in that chic and modern vibe we're going for.

ABOVE Arak Kanofsky Studios created these little citrus-shaped escort cards; I love how literal they are. The name of each guest adorns a different fruit, while the table number can be found on the attached leaf. For a surprise, slide the top slice off to reveal the juicy pulp inside.

USING CITRUS FRUITS TO DECORATE YOUR DINNER TABLE

- It's important to use a wide variety of citrus fruits so that the table feels fun and interesting. Just throwing a few bags of oranges down will not give you the same effect.

- The secret to making this look great is the variation, both in size and color, of the fruits: big grapefruits, mandarin oranges, kumquats, oranges, and lemons.

- Use fruit both on and off the branch; this allows you to utilize grocery store fruits as well as local, fresh-picked varieties.

- If you have trouble finding fruit still on the branch, try using camellia or gardenia foliage as a great way to bring in some green. Both mimic citrus leaves nicely.

- Create a freestyle runner of fruit down the center of a beautiful wooden table, layering all the different types together in a natural way. Remember, round fruit will roll, so take care with your placement.

- Make sure all the fruit is free from obvious blemishes and bruising. You wouldn't buy wilting flowers, so don't use past-their-prime fruits. And wash them! Your guests might grab a piece as a snack, so make sure the fruit is clean.

RIGHT Many of my clients assume that to set a beautiful table, you must use flowers, but I heartily disagree. Here I've put together a table featuring just the natural beauty of our inspirational citrus fruits. Consider using some round placemats in your palette instead of a decorative charger plate; the effect is casual and fun. They help to bring some color out from the center of the table as well. The final—and important—touch is the lanterns. They add some much-needed height that otherwise would be totally lacking with a citrus-only display.

These little place cards masquerading as lemon slices are great fun. Arak Kanofsky Studios did a lovely job creating them. Orange-colored calligraphy by Nancy Howell lets each guest know just where he or she belongs.

OPPOSITE I had two goals for this bouquet: The first was to play up the vibrant citron green color and the second was to create an absolutely crazy and over-the-top cascading shape. To achieve this, I began by layering the foliage and ferns, creating a kind of bed for the flowers to rest on. The long, cascading orchids came next; I let these flowers be my guide, allowing the shape of the bouquet to flow with the natural curves of the orchid stems. Once the heavier things were in place, I layered in some delicate velvety celosia for a bit of softness, and some orange *Sandersonia* for a hint of color; I love how the little *Sandersonia* blossoms look similar to kumquats. To keep it all together, I tied off the stems using two complementary ribbons: a skinny striped variety and a wider white grosgrain. A bouquet like this is best paired with a simple dress.

THIS PAGE A trio of desserts is a sweet way to bring an end to any meal. Marcey Brownstein Catering & Events came up with three sorbets. First, an orange sorbet with chocolate-covered candied sunflower seeds. Next, a lemon sorbet with slices of candied ginger. And finally, a lime sorbet featuring sugared kumquats.

OPPOSITE I arranged this bouquet tightly because I wanted to emphasize the tonal relationship of the flowers rather than the shape. From the poppies and tree peonies to the calla lilies and kangaroo paw, all of the flowers featured here share a wonderful painterly quality that I find really special.

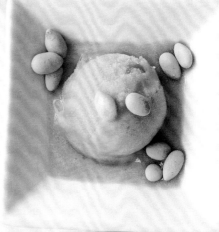

I.

-SALAD OF-

Blood Orange, Dates,
Parmesan & Almonds

II.

Wild Mushroom & Herb Tart

FORAGED MUSHROOMS, HERBS AND GRUYERE

Caneros District St. Clair Vineyard, Pinot Noir

EVA AND JONATHAN
Napa Valley
MAY 28, 2011

III.

Pan Roasted Veal Chop
with Silk Han kerchiefs

MUSTARD-COATED VEAL
MORELS, ASPARAGUS & LEMON
WITH HAND-CUT PASTA

IV.

Local Cheese Cart
Artisan Breads

BRIDE'S PICK: CYPRESS GROVE HUMBOLT FOG
GROOM'S PICK: FISCALINI BANDAGED CHEDDAR

V.

Individual Orange Soufflé

SERVED IN A VALENCIA ORANGE SHELL

Essensia, Quady Winery, Orange Muscat

WANT TO INCORPORATE CITRUS INTO YOUR MENU? HERE'S HOW

- Greet your guests with a refreshing glass of lemonade as they arrive for the ceremony; it's the perfect way to keep them cool on a warm summer day.
- Serve a citrus-infused drink during cocktail hour.
- Have your caterer create a few citrus-flavored sorbets that can be passed during cocktail hour, served as a deliciously appropriate palate cleanser throughout the meal, or presented as a refreshing dessert.
- Before you choose your caterer, talk to them about your inspiration, be it an easily incorporated one like citrus, or a more abstract one like the English pitcher (more on that later). Pick a few different caterers and ask them to create a tasting around your theme. That way, you'll get a chance to see who is seriously inventive. While squeezing a bit of lemon over a piece of salmon is yummy, it doesn't showcase culinary creativity.
- Consider serving a yummy soufflé or a sorbet right inside an orange shell. If you want to incorporate this idea into something savory, try filling the "fruit cup" with a citrus-infused couscous or quinoa.
- Of course, a lemon-flavored wedding cake would be delicious.
- You can even carry the theme through into brunch the next morning by serving lemon curd and scones to your guests.

LEFT   I've always admired the classic botanical drawings featured in horticultural textbooks; they have a wonderful scientific quality to them. So when it came time to create a citrus-inspired menu with Arak Kanofsky Studios, I knew right away that I wanted to feature that same type of illustration. I was quite happy with the way they turned out; they are fresh and bright. The stationer even thought to number each course using roman numerals, the traditional way to treat botanicals.

OPPOSITE   Ice pops are a delectable treat when it's hot outside, so if your event is set to take place during the dog days of summer, consider serving up these cool desserts. Offering a mini pop is a great way to bring some relief without risking a melty mess; stick to a smaller size, and don't forget to have plenty of napkins nearby! You could have a few waiters pass them around on platters at the start of a cocktail hour. They would also be great as the final sweet of the evening, served up in ice-filled enamel buckets where guests can grab them on their way out. These all-organic citrus-inspired treats came from Go-Go Pops in Cold Spring, New York.

OPPOSITE This table has a great vintage bistro vibe; it's warm and inviting. To achieve this look, I started with a white cloth as the base and then worked with these unique little orange trays, using them like mini-chargers. I folded a crisp white linen napkin to fit perfectly in a tray and then tied each one up like a cute little package with some orange twine. In an effort to keep things simple, I created just one lush centerpiece. This combination of flowers and ferns feels surprisingly effortless, considering how many of them are packed into this metal vase. There are bright orange daylilies and lacecap hydrangeas, peachy 'Sweet Juliet' roses, ferns, and a few other interesting things I found growing in the garden. I chose this bell-shaped stemware because it felt just right. Finally, I brought in brown bentwood chairs that fit in perfectly with the vintage bistro vibe.

ABOVE The crisp orange-meets-white color palette of this arrangement reminds me of places like Italy and Greece, where citrus fruits thrive and sun-bleached landscapes abound. I love the contrast between this clean, modern vessel and the busy, textural arrangement. I filled this urn with crab apple branches, *Gloriosa* lilies, and viburnum. A piece of this size works as an accent arrangement, a lovely addition to your seating-card table, or a beautiful welcome at the entrance to your ceremony.

ABOVE A welcome gift, like this thoughtful one designed by Gifts for the Good Life, could await your guests upon arrival in their hotel rooms. The faint, sun-bleached quality of this whole display is enticing; it reminds me of a destination wedding in Napa, just as the label suggests. Everything, from the citrus crate to the flavored sodas and candy, relates perfectly to our juicy citrusy inspiration.

What you'll find inside: Limonada—Two bottles of this sparkling lemonade make a cool, refreshing treat. To aid in your guests' enjoyment, they'll find two straws decorated with little citrus leaves, echoing the welcoming sentiments of the gift. *Citrus basil candle in a tin*—This fragrant candle will fill your guests' hotel rooms with a delightful scent and warm glow. Once they're home, it will remind them of that special time spent celebrating your love. *Citrus bath salts*—I adore how they packaged these bath salts in a diner-style sugar shaker! *Marzipan clementines*—These classic treats add a nice sweet contrast to the more tart lemony flavors. They're adorable too! *Candies*—The lemon-and-lime twists add some visual flavor. *Leone pastilles*—These famous little digestives come from Turin, Italy, where they've been a favorite of European royalty since the 1800s. Your noble guests will savor their lemon and lime flavors as well.

RIGHT This bouquet reminds me of the wildflowers you might find growing in the Napa Valley, or perhaps in picturesque Italy. I kept things free and loosely gathered for this combination of wild grasses, *Rudbeckia* (the sunflowerlike bloom), rosemary, dahlias, and *Asclepias*. The sunny palette shines through, making it a lovely complement to any citrus-inspired event. I love how fresh and handpicked this bouquet looks.

- Lanterns have many wonderful uses, and luckily are easy to rent.
- They add a magical glow without having to fuss with a lot of fancy lighting.
- Lanterns can be repurposed throughout the evening with barely any effort at all. They can start out lighting the path to your ceremony, get moved quickly over to the cocktail area next, and then finish off the night by guiding your guests back to their vehicles.
- They come in a wide variety of styles, colors, and sizes, making it easy to find a set that will complement your décor perfectly.

LEFT A charming pathway beckons. I love the metal-capped wooden lanterns pictured here; they add presence to this brick path.

OPPOSITE These orange-colored and -flavored specialty sodas poking out of white enamel buckets make for a great outdoor treat. A moment like this is perfect for a more casual event, or a rehearsal dinner leading up to your citrus-inspired wedding. I think it's nice when a wedding and rehearsal dinner relate, so if you find yourself with more ideas than you can use on your big day, work a few in on the night before.

PAINT-BY-NUMBERS

Why Paint-by-Number Paintings?

I've always been fascinated by the color palettes used in paint-by-number paintings; they tend to be both awkward and interesting. A lifelong friend who knows of my love for this wacky art form gifted these two paintings to me. I adore how these little canvases are trying so hard to be sophisticated still-life paintings.

Several years of art school left me with a sincere passion for creating still-life vignettes; I didn't realize then just how much that passion would influence my future work. I've found that the best way to pull together the overriding style for any event is to bring together a bunch of different objects that you love and then play around with them, in effect creating your own personalized still life. When you see all of these individual pieces come together as a whole, you can quickly get an idea of the style of event that would feel unique to you. It's a wonderful way to jump-start the creative process.

What About the Palette?

I'm inspired by the untraditional feel of these colors. The palette of gray and cream with a splash of coral is special—it is vintage, yet chic, making it a versatile jumping-off point.

Who Is the Client?

This inspiration is for the couple that loves to collect interesting objects—anything from stamps to books to ceramic pieces or old photographs. These ideas are perfect for the person who has acquired dozens and dozens of vintage dinner plates over the years, enough so there is one for each guest. Or this motif would suit someone who has amassed a lovely collection of china teapots and can create centerpieces from them for each table. This approach is definitely for the eclectic bride or groom who appreciates pieces that have their own history.

Where and When?

When I think about this unique inspiration, I imagine a wonderful farm wedding in a big old barn, or even a wedding at home with the guests milling around on a big wraparound porch. A cozy lodge or even an old castle would be a fantastic setting as well. The muted color palette makes me think of late summer moving into fall, when nature has begun its stunning transition.

My Focus

My focus here is to explore this slightly over-the-top, eclectic style and to bring to life the idea that not every event has to be designed around the same three colors, or two types of flowers, and so on. I also enjoy working with objects, either instead of, or along with, flowers to create a beautiful table setting. This approach is much more fun and unpredictable. I also want to offer up ideas for the couple that truly wants to personalize their wedding, creating an event like no other.

COLOR

I adore the untraditional palette represented in these little paintings. The gray, cream, and splash of coral feel vintage and chic, making them the perfect jumping-off point.

SHAPE/FORM

Creating little vignettes along your table or in a special nook is quite similar to pulling together a still life for a painting. I employ this concept in almost every event I design.

MOOD

I'm drawn to the slightly over-the-top, eclectic feeling of these two paintings. As inspiration, they proved to be extremely versatile and genuinely fun.

HUNTED AND GATHERED

OPPOSITE Drawn to the still-life quality of vintage paint-by-number pieces, I found myself choosing objects that could have easily been found in an old traditional artwork. I'm intrigued by the antiqued, almost subdued palette that's happening in the paintings as well. However, I freshened it up just a bit by adding in a few bold colors here and there.

LASER-CUT LINENS—I adore the color of this linen; the muted taupe and intricate laser-cut pattern have such a fantastic vintage air to them. Fabric like this is great for bringing in a pattern without introducing too many colors.

PEONIES—This coral pink color mixed in with this rather muted palette is sensational.

LAMB'S EARS—The soft and frosty texture of these leaves is quite appealing.

SAGE—The purple hue of this herb is a wonderful contribution to this palette.

BOOKS—They make fantastic decorative objects and can also help build height wherever you may need it.

RIBBON—The width of this ribbon is great; it gives it a lot of presence, and the creamy gold color is warm and lovely.

VINTAGE TROPHY—As a stand-alone object or a vessel for flowers, this antique trophy is great fun.

MINI BLACKBOARD—There is so much you can do with an object like this; you could display a table number on it or even use it as a quirky little tray.

GRAIN SCOOP—This vintage grain scoop is worn out beautifully and makes a unique container.

SMALL PITCHER—The peony makes this little guy tough to see, but stay tuned and you'll spot this "foxy" little pitcher later on.

ABOVE This bouquet highlights the softer creams and coral oranges featured in our inspirational paintings. The combination of *Ranunculus*, garden roses, and *Celosia* is so intense and stimulating that it's hard to believe there are so few floral varieties featured here. Orange and cream with gray is a chic and elegant color palette so I accessorized this bouquet with an exquisite floppy silk ribbon in a matte gray tone.

ABOVE I always enjoy gray and cream together—the combination is wonderfully vintage and soft. This table setting is simple and elegant, and a nice, unfussy interpretation of our paint-by-numbers inspirational paintings. Though you'll commonly find round tables at most event venues, think about using a square option like I did here. This shape affords your guests the same conversation opportunities, but feels more modern and fresh. To cover the table, I selected this tablecloth in a crisp, cool gray tone.

I had a local seamstress make napkins from this great striped fabric in yellow, cream, and gray. Napkins are easy to customize; they don't require a lot of fabric and are not difficult to sew. Do stick to linen or cotton if you're making your own, however, as slippery fabrics like satin or silk have a tendency to smear foods. Napkins are an important decorative element, but they still need to function as napkins!

Forgoing a charger plate, I folded our custom napkins into large squares and laid them at each place setting. Silver flatware feels special when paired with gray, so I chose a simple design to complement our more sparse table design. I chose these beautiful water glasses and wineglasses for their elegant bell-like shape. When creating a lush central floral arrangement like this, you should use a vessel that lifts it up and off the table a bit. Also remember that the vessel is the frame for your flowers, so give them somewhere beautiful to live for the night. I chose a creamy ceramic urn and then filled it with gray-blue hydrangeas as well as creamy tree peonies and garden roses, lambs' ears, and a touch of sage, all creating a lovely vintage feeling.

These white-washed Chiavari chairs are the perfect finishing touch; they too have a wonderful vintage feel to them.

DECORATING WITH FOOD

- A look like this is better suited for summer, as fruits and vegetables are at their freshest and most beautiful. If the tomatoes have to journey all the way from the southern hemisphere, it's doubtful they'll be perfect enough to serve as your décor.

- Remember to choose foods that vary in color, shape, and texture to create an interesting spread. Of course you want the food to taste yummy, but if it doesn't look beautiful and decorative, the effect is lost.

- Stick to side dishes and tasty breads for your décor, and plan to have the main dish plated and served.

- It's best to choose foods that taste yummy at room temperature, as things might sit out for a bit before your guests are ready to dig in.

- Don't go too crazy with foods that aren't meant to be eaten; it's better to fill the table with tasty things your guests can actually enjoy.

- For a large catered event, you definitely need to have a run-through with your caterer. You want to make sure that all the foods they plan to offer are attractive and easy for your guests to serve themselves. Take this time to run through the serving pieces as well, and make sure that each bowl and platter enhances the look of your table.

- Map out the table and have a plan in place for where each dish and delectable will go. You want to carefully orchestrate the design here, not toss a bunch of stuff down and walk away. Make sure that the entire waitstaff knows just where things go, and work with your caterer to ensure that nothing gets put out too early.

- If you're worried about pesky pests or the elements, try covering the food with mesh or metal domes. Both will offer protection, as well as provide a fun reveal for your guests once they sit down.

- Keep in mind that your décor is going to get eaten. Make sure to choose smaller serving vessels that can easily be replaced by the waitstaff, ensuring that the table will always appear full of food.

- Don't worry that your guests will end up sitting around an empty table once the meal is finished; people have a penchant for doing just that, while talking and enjoying themselves.

- If you're bothered by an empty setting, have a few small flower arrangements ready to go once the food has been cleared away. Another way to fill the space is a full coffee and tea service tray; one could be brought out for each table, letting your guests enjoy as many mugs as they'd like.

PREVIOUS SPREAD, LEFT Flowers will always be my first love, I admit it. However, that does not mean that I think they're the only option for tabletop décor. Food can make for a beautiful and interactive centerpiece. I collaborated closely with Marcey Brownstein Catering & Events to create this delectable spread. To start, I laid down a striped fabric runner to create the base of our food-filled setting. I chose something beautiful that would remain once everything else had been devoured. It's important for your guests to have a cutting surface, so use wooden cutting boards like I did here; they're practical, yet perfect for displaying foods, especially breads. In addition to the cutting boards, I brought in tiny wooden stools to create a bit of height. Now to the food: The long, crispy black sesame and sea salt flatbread serves as an edible runner. The beet, carrot, and whole-grain tricolor couscous not only looks beautiful with its many colors, but tastes great at room temperature too. Notice how the vibrant tomatillo, peach, tomato, and basil salad is as much a feast for the eyes as it is for the palate. And the roasted cauliflower peeking in from the right is gorgeous! One of my favorite offerings is the red and green Cerignola olives—the colors really pop, especially in that white bowl. The breadsticks add texture and variation to the rustic and bountiful display. To finish, we placed many of the vegetable ingredients found in the meal around the table to layer in more shapes and color.

OPPOSITE I love working with orchids; nothing is quite like their exotic nature and stunning color combinations. Here I planted a few varieties in vintage pewter pots to create a charming still-life vignette at the center of this dining table. The stunner in the middle is called a lady slipper orchid—it was so filled with personality, I half expected it to whisper something to me. The variety on the right is known as a *Vanda* orchid, while the other two are different styles of miniature *Phalaenopsis*.

If orchids are out of your price range, consider potting up herbs, hydrangeas, or pansies for a similar style. Any bulb flower will work perfectly well: Tulips are inexpensive in the spring and are still a classic beauty.

I covered the table with this gorgeous gray fabric that felt almost like super-refined burlap and then used some silver accents to play up the tone. Stemless glassware added a clean modern touch, while Moroccan tea votives lent a nice warm glow to the setting. I layered a simple off-white plate atop a pewter charger and let the napkins drape over the side of the table.

CREATING AN ENTIRELY OBJECT-BASED TABLE

- An approach like this can work well for a dinner party at home and even a large-scale event like a wedding. Obviously a single table would be easier to pull together, as the number of objects needed is greatly reduced. However, if you give yourself enough time, you can manage to acquire enough pieces to cover a large grouping of tables. For a wedding, start scouring flea markets, yard sales, and vintage shops about a year in advance. Check Etsy and eBay too!

- If you live in or nearby a large city, search for a prop house; they will likely have an endless supply of wacky and wonderful objects from which to choose.

- Remember, you want to create a setting easy and pleasant for the eye to travel over; make sure to use objects that vary in height, size, shape, and color.

- You want this to feel interesting and playful, not overwhelming and strange, so keep the mood of your objects the same. Here I worked with vintage, muted pieces, but the options are endless.

- If you're putting together multiple tables, choose one or two unifying objects to tie them all together. For example, if I were expanding this setting, I might use books and feathers on all and then play around with the rest of the pieces. You could swap out the horse head on the next table over for a large metal bird, and replace the vintage wooden bowling pins for fun pool balls. As long as all the objects have a similar playfulness and palette, I think you can just go wild!

- Let the objects be your guide when choosing flatware, glasses, and plates; try to keep them simple so that your still-life runner remains the focal point. I accented the décor with these narrow glasses from Roost that have delicate botanical designs etched into them. Clean silver flatware and a folded napkin complete the setting. As a small token, each guest will find a mirrored matchbox to take home.

- Let your table number be another place to have some fun. The vintage chalkboard from among our inspirational objects was the perfect fit for this table. Consider displaying the number differently on each table—look for large numbers while you're out hunting and gathering.

LEFT I absolutely love this table. I know it's a bit eccentric, but you could certainly rein it in if you'd like. I wanted to give an example of an entirely object-based table setting—devoid of flowers—the ultimate still-life table, if you will.

THIS PAGE The painterly palette of these carnations is dreamy. People tend to think this old standby can't be chic, but looking at these amazing taupe-and-salmon-pink–hued beauties, I beg to differ. This variegated variety plays off of our muse perfectly, making this bouquet a fun choice for our paint-by-numbers event.

USING A SPECIAL PIECE TO CREATE A SPECIAL MOMENT

- When you find yourself with interesting little spaces to fill, think about featuring special pieces—perhaps a vase from your mother's collection, or your grandmother's favorite family heirloom.

- Was there a delicate teapot you were allowed to use to carefully host teddy bear–attended parties? If so, pull it out of retirement and find a place to show it off.

- Just remember to make certain that these family heirlooms make their way back to you once the festivities have drawn to a close. In the hustle and bustle of a big cleanup, things can end up in the wrong hands, so remind your rental company which items are yours. Place a sticker or sticky note on the bottom of each of your items just to be sure, and put a friend in charge of collecting the pieces at the end of the evening.

- If you're afraid to include your own things, or just don't have anything that suits, accent pieces are good things to spend a little time and money on. They are meant to draw the eye, so give them their due. Scour your favorite local shops and flea markets for a few items that will stand out, but remember that you will own them, so take into account whether they might work their way into your daily life or not. If they do not, consider giving away any special pieces as gifts after the big day. Your new mother-in-law and your favorite aunt may love having something that brings back memories of your wedding or event.

LEFT   These wonderful wooden palettes designed by Arak Kanofsky Studios are playful; I love how literal they are. With the thumbhole acting as the perfect napkin ring, and the painted name as a seating card, all your place-setting needs are taken care of with one whimsical accessory. A cute choice like this would work perfectly for a casual daytime event, or perhaps for a children's table at a larger wedding.

OPPOSITE   Here's that little piece from our inspirational objects photograph. The fox adorning this glazed English pitcher is so sweet that I had to put him front and center. I laid down an off-white double-hemstitched napkin as a frame for this special moment and then gave the whole arrangement some height by placing it on top of these delicate little books. I worked with mock orange, orchids, *Celosia*, *Ranunculus*, and fragrant mint to create this tiny painterly arrangement. Use it alone as a sweet accent or build up an entire table setting by making lots of similar arrangements in varying heights.

RIGHT Once again, I created a beautiful still life at the center of this table. I wanted to show how using found objects, rather than vases and bowls, can be a fantastic way to show off flowers. Remember that laser-cut cloth from our inspirational objects? I've laid it down here to give the table some visual interest that won't compete with our still-life display. The warm tone of the cloth underneath peaks through the taupe runner, bringing life to the cut-out design. This combination lends a nice country note to the setting without feeling too down-home.

I bring in interesting flatware whenever a setting can support it: These dark wooden-handled forks, spoons, and knives contribute nicely to the chic country vibe. I kept the plates simple and topped them with rolled napkins secured with bits of grosgrain ribbon and vintage velvet flowers.

If you can place a glass liner inside, any unique object can be become a vessel worthy of holding flowers. I like using pieces that feel a bit wacky; it's more interesting when the vessel itself is just as creative as the arrangement inside.

Left to right: A small wire basket holding two little milk bottles. Inside the bottles there's a mixture of baby tulips, sage, and small *Phalaenopsis* orchids. A fantastic old grain scoop with peonies, mint, and mock orange inside. A rustic old toolbox, which made the perfect planter, filled with rich purple hydrangeas and geranium foliage. A tall "vase," which is actually a candle mold that I filled with orchids. I love the dramatic bit of height created by this arrangement. An old flour sifter, in which you'll find a mixture of peonies, mock orange, and mint, echoing the grain scoop at the other end of the table.

ABOVE A long, thin table, like the chrome-plated one pictured here, makes a great altar piece. I simply covered it with glass hurricanes containing creamy pillar candles, which create a fantastic warm glow when lit. I tucked in large lamb's ear leaves to soften the lines of the table and give the whole display a bit of poetry. You could also use tropical leaves, ferns, vines, or even go the more traditional route and use petals.

OPPOSITE I strove for a painterly quality in this bouquet. I used romantic blooms and then tweaked the whole nosegay with muted succulents. The subtle pink edging on the succulents' leaves is perfectly matched with the bright pink peonies and sweet pea. The purple sage and feathery textural elements turn up the vintage volume in a wonderful way. This wide, coppery brown double-faced satin ribbon is the perfect finishing touch.

THIS PAGE The soft shape of these pink calla lilies looks just like a paintbrush waiting to dance across a canvas. I used them as an accent to the creamy peonies, rather than having a mass of lilies that blend together. I added gray dusty miller around the base to bring in a touch of that great neutral color.

OPPOSITE This accent piece is simple, yet it speaks volumes about our inspiration. To set the stage, I worked with two striped runners, layering them on to create this great linear effect. I filled the old mottled trophy with geraniums and peonies and left it at that. I love how uncomplicated the whole display looks.

FRENCH CANDY

Why French Candy?

I've noticed that people love to collect candy when they travel. I have a friend who brings back a special chocolate bar from each trip he takes. How people don't devour their sweet treats long before they've gotten home, I don't know, but collecting them is certainly a lovely sentiment. Even if your favorite foreign confection didn't survive the long journey back, consider turning to whatever it was that you fancied as a uniquely personal inspirational object.

What About the Palette?

Wouldn't it be lovely to send your guests home with a favor filled with your inspiration? One thing I really love about these candies is their color. Of course the sweet pinks are a great jumping-off point, but what makes this palette feel more sophisticated is the lemony yellow and muted orange and green tones. Candy can be quite garish, let's be honest, with its often painfully bright and cheeky colors, but these French berlingots are the exact opposite. They're elegant and lovely and they instantly transport me to the fanciful candy shops of Paris.

Who Is the Client?

This inspiration is especially for the couple looking for something classically pretty and sweet. These ideas are perfect for the person who loves delicate details, like a beautiful ribbon tied around a lovely favor, the elegant hemstitch on a perfectly pressed napkin, and the soft petals of a beautiful peony tucked inside a bouquet.

Where and When?

I think the slightly more ornate vibe and all the lovely pastel tones in this palette lend themselves to a winter or spring wedding. A traditional and embellished ballroom would be perfect for this type of inspiration—think Marie Antoinette! An urban loft could work as well, creating a nice contrast between a more masculine space and a decidedly more feminine décor.

My Focus

Those dreamy faraway Parisian boutiques I mentioned earlier were the impetus for this chapter. I want to play up the whimsical feeling that you get upon entering one. With their gilded décor and decadent offerings, you can't help but feel like, well, a kid in a candy store! I also want to give you some ideas on how to work with a very traditional palette, like soft pink and white, and yet still maintain a unique, unfussy, and contemporary aesthetic.

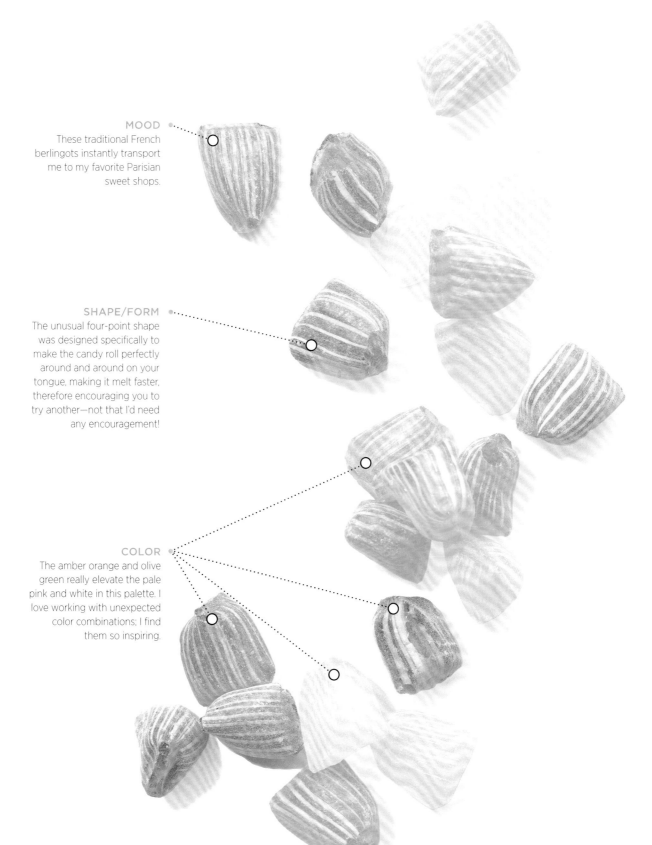

MOOD
These traditional French berlingots instantly transport me to my favorite Parisian sweet shops.

SHAPE/FORM
The unusual four-point shape was designed specifically to make the candy roll perfectly around and around on your tongue, making it melt faster, therefore encouraging you to try another—not that I'd need any encouragement!

COLOR
The amber orange and olive green really elevate the pale pink and white in this palette. I love working with unexpected color combinations; I find them so inspiring.

HUNTED AND GATHERED

OPPOSITE You can see easily that this palette is mostly pink and cream, but I wanted to make sure that those pops of amber and green were incorporated as well. They're a great way to tweak what could become an overly sweet color scheme. My goal is to create an eclectic vibe that focuses on the sweet, pink, perfect candy shop, but also gives equal play to the elegant, warm, yet historical feel that's present in some of the older Parisian shops.

GILDED COOKIE JAR—Don't you just want to know what homemade treats await you inside?

BELL'OCCHIO BOXES—These adorable boxes come from a great specialty shop in San Francisco.

QUILLING PAPER—Great for embellishing packages.

GILDED WALLPAPER SAMPLES FROM GRAHAM & BROWN—The gilded detail reminds me so much of the pattern in the candy

MOTHER-OF-PEARL BUTTONS IN A JAR—These come from Tinsel Trading, one of my favorite shops in New York City. My friend Marcia Ceppos, whose family has been collecting trims and goodies for generations, owns the store.

INDIAN FABRIC NAPKINS—With their elegant gilded pattern, these napkins from ABC Home in New York City were a lucky find. Fancy and delicate, they call the candy to mind.

VINTAGE PINK MILK GLASS CANDY DISHES—My grandmother had something just like these when I was young.

WRAPPING PAPER—I was instantly drawn to the great wafflelike texture of this paper.

WALLPAPER—That background might look like real bead board, but don't be fooled—it's wallpaper. I love that it mimics the subtle striping in the candy

DONUTS AND CUPCAKES—The candied sprinkles on these delicious mini donuts and the frosting on the cupcake are perfectly in palette—yum!

RIBBONS AND EMBROIDERY THREADS—Soft pinks and greens for those finishing touches.

GILDED PITCHER—The layering of the pink, gold, and white pattern drew me to it; it has a French fabulousness that makes it irresistible.

- It's often less expensive than specialty fabrics, making it easier to dress things up on a budget.
- It's more convenient than fabric because the width of a typical roll of wallpaper or wrapping paper is much more manageable, requiring less time and work. Fabric often has to be cut and sewn to create a nice runner, whereas rolled paper needs just two precise cuts.
- One thing to keep in mind if you decide to use wallpaper: Stick to styles that are not backed with adhesive. The odor of the glue may unpleasantly interfere with dinner, especially if it's hot outside.
- Another thing that's great about paper—no ironing!

LEFT Instead of putting treats in jars and on cake stands, I displayed the sweets on these great hat, shirt, and letter boxes from Bell'occhio. They have a special wafflelike texture that plays right into our candy theme. Have fun with this idea by opening up the lids and letting the sweets overflow onto the table. Not only is this presentation more inviting and playful, it brings in the color palette beautifully. Underneath the boxes I rolled out a wallpaper runner that reminded me of pulled taffy. I designed the whole table to have a very fancy yet graphic quality, where the old world and the modern come together perfectly.

Including cookies is a wonderful way to further personalize the whole affair. Ask your favorite neighborhood bakery or cookie shop to supply the treats; you don't have to rely solely on your caterer or cake designer. Make sure to include some of each partner's favorite recipes. You can even ask family members and friends to contribute by having them make one of their specialties that you love. Most important, have fun with a display like this—don't limit yourself!

DESSERT HOUR

- Instead of serving dessert back at the dinner table, I love the idea of creating a separate, special area for just that purpose. Invite your guests to enjoy the final course away from their tables, which will allow them to mingle with those they did not share dinner with, and perhaps give them the chance to see another part of your venue.

- Set smaller, more intimate, tables with unexpected chocolate pots, elegant mugs, and a bowl filled with fresh marshmallows.

- You can stick to the traditional poured coffee service, or you can place the coffee pots right on the tables, allowing your friends and family to pour their own.

- Consider including small candy dishes filled with unique cookies to give those who don't relish cake something to snack on as well.

- If you find yourself short on space, simply repurpose the cocktail hour area.

- China chocolate pots aren't exactly a staple on most registries today, but they used to be the mark of a good hostess—ready for anything her company might desire. You should have no trouble finding them in antique and vintage shops, as well as at local flea markets. Don't think you need to acquire enough matching pots to cover all your tables—it's better to find pieces that work in harmony together but that contribute to a more eclectic look. Remember that you can mix vintage and modern styles together; nothing has to match as long as it looks good as a whole!

LEFT These meringues and cookies from One Girl Cookies in New York City wonderfully convey that Parisian sweet-shop feel that I was going for. I love the way they look on these Bell'occhio boxes. Not only does the waferlike texture work perfectly with the sweets theme, the color palette of the boxes echoes that of the inspirational French candies beautifully. To set the sweets table, I used a paper runner that reminded me of the pulled taffy you might find while visiting the shore on the East Coast.

OPPOSITE Once dinner has been cleared, thoughts will inevitably turn to coffee and sweets. Whether you decide to have one large cake or an entire dessert table, consider making a slightly bigger production out of it than tradition calls for. Typically, the happy couple stands, knife in hand by the cake, surrounded by friends and family, to make the first slice together. Everyone smiles and laughs as the couple feeds each other a bite and then they head back to their respective tables to await a small piece of cake. Why not mix things up a bit?

THIS PAGE This round bouquet features hot pink peonies tightly packed together with some soft pink hydrangeas and double lisianthus. The vibrant color of these peonies is divine; this is pink at its sexiest. The chenillelike *Amaranthus* and the curling passion vine add a romantic, decadent feeling.

sweet love

THIS PAGE A box, like this one from Modern Press, can be uniquely personalized. It's great as a welcome gift for a destination wedding or could even be used as part of the turn-down service in your guests' hotel rooms on the night of your wedding. It makes a great takeaway favor as well for a treat on the run.

RIGHT I was drawn to this invitation by Modern Press Stationery because it's a great modern interpretation of something very girly and sweet. I love the laser-cut flowers that decorate the card. They remind me of sugared violets, a wonderful little nod to our sweets inspiration. There's a lot of layering here, which gives this invitation wonderful dimension. From the outside in, the whole "gift" starts with an address band that guides the invite to its rightful recipient. The band wraps tightly around a package that invokes the candy boxes of old. Inside, two tones of pink paper envelope the card; open them up to reveal this lovely letterpress offer to attend your wedding. The invitation itself is layered on top of pink paper, allowing the flower cutouts to really jump out at you.

together with our families
we invite you to celebrate our marriage
saturday . the first of may . two thousand ten . two o'clock in the afternoon
the new york botanical gardens . new york city
festivities to follow

tessa regan chandross and jack clark nelson

Jenn and Kyle

Denise and Will Holden

Neal Griffin

LEFT These lovely escort cards by Modern Press Stationery feature the same dahlia-inspired floral pattern as the custom coasters and invitations at right.

SAVETHEDATE

04 22

AMANDA BRIGHTON AND W

THE HONOUR OF YOUR PRESENCE
IS REQUESTED AT THE MARRIAGE OF

AMANDA NICOLE BRIGHTON
AND **WILLIAM LAWRENC**

ON SATURDAY, THE TWENTY-SECOND OF
TWO THOUSAND TEN
AT HALF PAST FOUR O'CLOCK IN THE A
THE PAVILLION AT SPRINGFIELD WEST
SPRINGFIELD

RECEPTION IMMEDIATELY FOLLOWING

CONSIDERING COASTERS

- Coasters are a fun and modern alternative to traditional paper cocktail napkins. You can have them in stacks sitting on your bar as well as a few on each cocktail table. Your bartender can even hand them out as he or she serves drinks to your guests.

- Most stationers will be happy to design and print a coaster that augments all your printed motifs.

- You can, of course, have your names and wedding date printed on them, just like you would a traditional cocktail napkin. However, consider working with just the imagery and leaving off the specifics. This allows you to use the coasters for future parties at home. These dahlia-dotted ones could work in any number of occasions, even your future daughter's first birthday party. Remember that you don't have to toss all those extras after the big day; repurpose them and save yourself money and time in the future—the earth will thank you, too!

- Coasters can also help introduce another pattern, and thus layer, to your décor. Go on the hunt for some great preprinted ones that will coordinate well with what you already have going on. Remember that it's the layering of textures, patterns, and colors that make things seem really special, so don't be afraid to add something new. Another pattern, as long as it lives in harmony with the other things you've chosen, will add a new dimension to the décor.

LEFT   Though I have mainly focused on a more old-fashioned candy shop vibe, here I show you how something more modern could work perfectly.

Modern Press Stationery designed a charming suite of printed materials, starting with the save-the-date mailer that features this wonderfully graphic dahlialike imagery. It's a clean, yet whimsical shape that reminds me of the quality displayed on our inspirational French treats. It's definitely modern, but it's playful and sweet, allowing the stationery to complement the more traditional accents I've gathered. Modern Press Stationery used that same motif on the invitations, escort cards, printed coasters, and even the menus that adorned each place setting.

LEFT Here's a great example of carrying your printed motifs through the whole wedding. This menu card features the dahlia design on both the menu itself as well as the contrasting pink sleeve covering it. I like pairing a menu card with a decorative napkin; the combination allows you to avoid other embellishments at the place setting. While I agree with most caterers that food should be presented on white plates, I do think you can have fun with a colorful charger. Poking out from underneath this lovely pink milk glass charger is a table runner made of wallpaper. The orange-gold hues featured in this print echo the amber color in the French candies perfectly.

OPPOSITE The candy color palette shines through in this classic garden bouquet. The lush 'Yves Piaget' and 'Sweet Juliet' roses combined with the white Tweedia and astilbe create this nice summery feeling. I played up the warmth of the orange-colored berlingot candies with the peach-toned roses. The little pops of white Tweedia add a touch of frostiness that reminds me of the stripes adorning our candies. I love how sweet and vibrant this feels.

STANDARD RENTALS

Remember, each element present on the reception tables is part of the overall look. Guests will notice the plates just as much as the flowers, so treat your rentals as a valuable part of the overall décor.

PLATES: While it is generally agreed that dinner should be served on a plain plate, that doesn't mean your entire setting has to be white and sterile.

- Ask your caterer or rental company about the basic package they offer, and then find out what it would cost to upgrade to a more decorative charger plate.
- Decorative china plates make a wonderful addition to any setting, either as a charger or a more festive salad or dessert plate. If you do decide to serve a salad on a more decorative dish, ask to see what the food looks like beforehand, just to make sure that the pattern won't overwhelm the food.
- Decorative china seems more special somehow. It conjures up childhood memories of holidays and special dinners with the family, so it's a wonderful addition to this special occasion.

FLATWARE: Flatware can be a great example of using a standard rental piece to dress up your table. Spoons, forks, and knives are obviously a must, so think of them as another opportunity to make a beautiful statement.

- The options are endless, from supersimple stainless steel to intricate and ornate vintage silver. Once again, check out what the basics are, and then ask about an upgrade.
- Stainless will generally be more affordable, but if you've dreamed of dining with genuine silver on your big day, then cut back on something else and splurge on the good stuff.
- I love mingling patterns; I think it's a wonderful way to bring more depth to the table. If you're hosting, say, one hundred and twenty guests, rent forty sets of three different styles, and ask your caterer to mix them up at each setting. One thing to keep in mind with the mixing: You shouldn't pair stainless with silver. The tones in the two metals are different enough that they won't complement each another.

NAPKINS: It's likely that your venue will offer a standard white linen napkin to match their standard white linen tablecloth, but don't let these staples slip by without giving it some consideration.

- A lovely napkin can make further embellishments unnecessary, so see what else your local rental company has to offer.
- Napkins can create a perfect packaging moment to finish off a place setting, either for your flatware, the menu, or even a lone blossom. I especially love the hemstitched ones featured here.

STEMWARE: As with the rest of your rented place setting, the choices are endless with stemware.

- Stemware is definitely one thing that most rental companies will have in spades, so take advantage of that.
- Everything from traditional cut-glass leaded crystal to more modern stemless versions are available, so be sure to look beyond the first option that's presented to you.
- If you do find yourself with limited options, look for one special glass, like a pretty colored water glass or a unique champagne flute. Even if you're only able to tweak one of the glasses, it will still have a big impact.

CHAIRS: There will be dozens, possibly hundreds, of chairs in your venue, so don't forget to consider their visual impact when choosing which ones to rent.

- It's easier to find more choices in urban environments, but don't let that deter you.
- Investigate what the venue has to offer—sometimes they might have a whole stack of chairs that they don't use anymore sitting down in the basement. They might have replaced them with these new, supposedly better chairs, but you may find the older chairs to be cooler. The rental company may even be willing to paint old chairs, so don't be afraid to ask!
- Different colors can say a lot about your table. If you have a really tight color palette, then perhaps a soft blue chair, for example, could be an amazing way to emphasize it.

OPPOSITE The painted white brick of this space makes it look like a room constructed entirely out of big, spongy marshmallows. It's the perfect example of using your setting to accent your theme. I tucked a Marie Antoinette–inspired pitcher into this little nook because I adore the juxtaposition of an urban, loftlike space with an item that feels plucked from the past. I filled the "vase" with some lovely Japanese lisianthus, a few soft pink peonies, parrot tulips, and creamy sweet pea flowers, forming a small, yet extremely lush, bouquet. The arrangement stood out in this gilded pitcher, taking it from just another bunch of flowers to a special moment waiting to be discovered. I scattered pink mercury glass votives around to bring out the color of both the flowers and the vessel.

FLOATING FLOWERS

- In lieu of using traditional flower arrangements, consider floating big blossoms in various-sized water-filled bowls to give them some room to breathe.
- The secret to making this look great is using large, open-faced flowers like these peonies and lisianthus. I added hydrangea florets to accent the larger blooms.
- The other trick is to mix up the shapes and sizes of your vessels. Don't forget to include different color tones as well. Here's another great opportunity to use items gathered from vintage shops and flea markets, so get creative with what you choose. Ask to peruse what your rental company has to offer; they may have a few different vessels (even soup bowls) that could work as well.
- If you're worried about your ability to pull it all together, try to work with one unifying theme. For example, make the vessels all one color but vary the shapes, or pick one shape and mix up the colors. Either way, you should remember to use several different sizes in your arrangement.
- Make sure you have some large focal pieces and then accent those with smaller bowls to make your table more interesting. And trust your instincts—if you don't think it looks good, then don't use it!

LEFT I know I keep talking about color, but it's true that you should let your palette be your guide—especially when it comes to piecing together your table setting. A pink tablecloth might seem a bit cutesy, but if you pick the right shade and pair it with an elegant white cotton runner, like I did here, you end up with a chic base for your table. I love the open weave of this runner, as it lets the pink peek through a bit. It's also a wonderful way of adding texture without going too crazy.

Remember to make the place setting decorative too. Everything on the table should be considered. A beautiful floral display will only look as good as what's around it, so pay attention to the charger plate, serving pieces, stemware, and glassware as well. Here, I started things off with a pearlescent glass charger plate topped with a simple white dinner plate. I tied some pink silk ribbon around the napkin to create a little package and then topped each one with some hydrangea blossoms. I added another layer of interest by varying the colors of the place cards—the ladies are greeted by a light pink version, while the gentlemen receive a more vibrant hot pink one.

LEFT If you're using a variety of flowers in the bride's bouquet, I think it's a great idea to stick to one type of blossom for each of the bridesmaids. It's a nice way to make them all feel special! Keeping the bouquets small allows you to make them lush, without making them pricey. I try to choose flowers that have interesting and different textures so that each one really does look unique. Here I decided on lisianthus, peonies, and parrot tulips, each accented with a complementary silk ribbon.

OPPOSITE My goal here is to take this preppy palette of pink and green and show how to tweak it by adding in peachy tones, thereby pushing it to a more unexpected place. This centerpiece of *Hydrangea paniculata* 'Grandiflora' (a more cone-shaped variety with smaller blossoms), white *Scabiosa*, peonies, and garden roses looks fresh inside this cool vintage urn. The *Scabiosa* adds some whimsy and helps to keep the whole arrangement from becoming too moundlike. I ringed the table with gold chairs to make things gleam just a bit.

LET THEM EAT CAKE!

Lately I find that couples want to focus more on lots of different sweets and treats, forgoing the traditional larger cake. I love this idea—I think it's certainly more fun and interesting to mix things up.

- A dessert table like this allows you to still have one larger, fancy cake, like the coconut one here, that you can cut with your new spouse, but doesn't limit you to a single choice.

- If you decide to have a wide selection, make sure you vary the heights and styles of the cakes and the stands and plates on which they sit. On our table the coconut cake is large, the chocolate is small, and the pistachio falls right in between, giving the eye somewhere to travel.

- You can bring in pops of color with serving pieces, like the pink glass plate on our table. Ask your close family and friends to see what cake stands and decorative plates they may have to lend; they will love to contribute to your event in such a fun way. And, of course, don't forget to check your local antique shops and flea markets to see what you can find. Etsy is another great source for mix-and-match vintage pieces. New cake stands and plates can obviously mix in beautifully as well.

- Cupcakes are great to include if you're inviting children to your event. They easily allow moms to exert portion control!

- Don't forget to include some of your childhood favorites. If your grandmother makes an amazing hummingbird cake, either ask her to whip one up, or instruct your caterer to use her recipe. This is a chance to further personalize your event, so take advantage of the opportunity.

- Let your guests serve themselves; it's definitely more fun. But do make sure there is enough to go around, just in case some people indulge in more than one slice!

RIGHT Let them eat cake! Or cupcakes, as it were. Two of our supercute flower girls, dressed in Ash & Robbins pink silk frocks, were totally busted munching on some sweets before it was time—but how can you blame them with a spread as tempting as this one? Here I've pulled together a dessert table featuring lots of old-fashioned cakes for people to choose from. Modern Press Stationery made up the lovely paper garland, which was strung up to declare just where the "Sweet Treats" could be found.

CONSIDERING OLD-FASHIONED CAKES

- Wedding cakes seem to be getting larger and more complicated every day, but you shouldn't feel as if it's important to top the last one you witnessed being cut. Smaller cakes are lovely and always less expensive. Your cake doesn't have to have as many layers as your dress—keep it simple and elegant.
- Consider buttercream for the icing, it's delicious.
- If you choose to do something old-fashioned like this, think about putting it on a lovely cloth to give it a more unique presence.
- Don't forget, if your cake has to sit on a board, make sure your baker covers it in something that works well with the style of your wedding. No cardboard showing through, please!

OPPOSITE Instead of going overboard, consider a smaller, traditional layer cake, like this beautiful confection from Sugar Sweet Sunshine. The pink frosting reminds me of soft petals sweeping across the cake. We nestled some peonies on top to make it extra special.

ABOVE A bento box is the perfect takeaway. I worked with Arak Kanofsky Studios to create this wonderful treat-filled version. We packed it full with lollipops, gourmet jelly beans, peach buttons, and delicious cookies (all in our palette, of course), but you could let your guests do the packing instead. Consider creating a delicious candy bar where your friends and family could fill up on a wide variety of treats at the end of the evening. It's a fun way to send them off into the night.

PORTUGUESE BEAD

Why This Portuguese Bead?

This little patterned bead was a gift from my dear friend and mentor Maria Vella. While traveling in Portugal, Maria spotted this trinket in a bead shop and picked it up with me in mind. She's always understood my love for and collection of whimsical little objects and knew right away that I would cherish this new addition instantly. Maria is the one who taught me to love and understand flowers. We'd spend hours walking in her mother's garden in Sonoma, where she would give me lessons on the different names and varieties of all the things growing there. She showed me that seeing a flower in its natural environment helps you to incorporate it more beautifully in an arrangement or bouquet: Once you know what the plant does naturally, you'll never want to force it to be something that it's not.

What About the Palette?

The vine motif winding its way around this bead feels lush, despite its delicate nature. It's exotic and tropical, yet somewhat reserved. I'm rather obsessed with the green and white color palette. It can be challenging to work within an extremely tight palette like this, but in general it forces you to be more creative and to dig a little deeper than you would have otherwise.

This ultrarefined palette of green and white is fresh. You'll be amazed at how much we can do with a seemingly limited range of tones. There's a wonderful boldness that happens when you allow green, which normally finds itself in a supporting role, to be paired with rich wood tones and crisp whites.

Who Is the Client?

My Portuguese bead makes me think of a couple that enjoy nature and are inspired by the outdoors. They love leaves, foliage, and maybe even viny and exotic plants, and would prefer their focus to be on the greener side of things, rather than on flowers.

Where and When?

A look like this can work just about anywhere, from an intimate backyard event to a lovely daytime affair, or even brought to life in a traditional ballroom. This inspiration can work in many settings, although spring and summer might be best, as the natural environment during fall and winter might really work against you. However, I wouldn't rule out an evergreen take on this theme during the snowy months.

My Focus

My focus with this chapter is to create an exotic and overgrown botanical vibe that can permeate its way into every minute detail. I want everything to feel incredibly lush, foresty, and secret garden–like, as if no one has tended the grounds of an old home in quite some time.

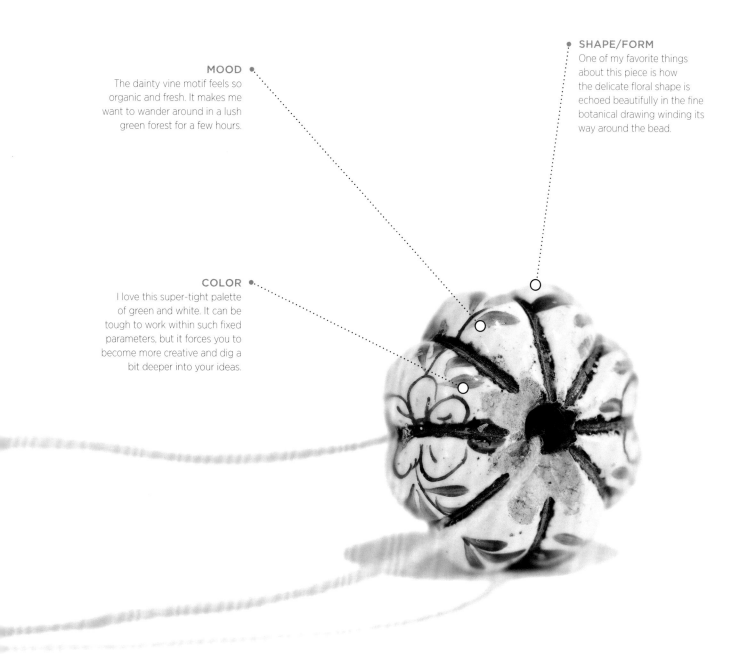

MOOD

The dainty vine motif feels so organic and fresh. It makes me want to wander around in a lush green forest for a few hours.

SHAPE/FORM

One of my favorite things about this piece is how the delicate floral shape is echoed beautifully in the fine botanical drawing winding its way around the bead.

COLOR

I love this super-tight palette of green and white. It can be tough to work within such fixed parameters, but it forces you to become more creative and dig a bit deeper into your ideas.

HUNTED AND GATHERED

OPPOSITE I'm in love with this palette; it's spare, but absolutely beautiful. The green against the white is crisp and yet lush. It might seem as if your options would be quite limited using just two colors, but you'll be surprised and delighted by how many options you have.

GREEN WATER GLASSES—I enjoy using one special colored glass in and among regular clear stemware; it has a wonderful effect on the table as a whole.

BEGONIA LEAVES—The pebbly texture of these leaves is fantastic.

FERNS AND SUCCULENTS—Although they generally inhabit different climates, ferns and succulents look beautiful alongside one another.

LILY OF THE VALLEY—This tiny flower is so fragrant, it makes for an amazing and sweet little bouquet.

PHALAENOPSIS ORCHIDS—Phalaenopsis orchids are chic and exotic; you can never go wrong by incorporating them into your design.

PRINTED DINNER NAPKINS—These stamped linen napkins, with their green, viny motif, would be the perfect accent for any bead-inspired table.

GREEN FOLIAGE WALLPAPER—The first thing I thought of when I saw this wallpaper was my Portuguese bead; it's so spot-on, it's almost as if it were designed just for this chapter.

GREEN-AND-WHITE ITALIAN PITCHER—This little pitcher is delicate and sweet.

FRENCH GROSGRAIN RIBBON—This bit of ribbon would be great for tying off a lovely little nosegay.

WHITE CERAMIC VOTIVES—I love the open stitch-like decoration on these votives; it allows the light to shine through and dance across the table.

BLACK-AND-WHITE-PATTERNED POTS—These vessels felt exotic to me; they're wonderfully earthy.

LEFT Oftentimes, the getting-from-here-to-there spaces at weddings end up being neglected. Decorating a long hallway or a simple garden path can be a lovely way to keep your guests engaged throughout the entire event. Here, I've strung up stunning gardenia blossoms to create not only a visual treat, but a fragrant one as well. As your guests walk through on their way to somewhere else, they can catch a sweet whiff and smile as they go.

OPPOSITE The goal here was to create a ceremony arch that felt alive, totally overgrown, and organic—inspired by the tropical rainforest, not a tropical beach. There are seven different varieties of *Tillandsia*, or air plants, displayed on this arch, all of which feel like they might get up and walk away if bothered in the slightest. You'll also find a few styles of fern, several different succulents, *Smilax*, and moss. Everything here is hardy and simply needs to be misted. You can build an arch like this the day before your event, making it a nice do-it-yourself option. I love how ours has a slight lean to the side—it adds to the organic quality. Arches not only generate a wonderful space under which to say your vows, but create a beautiful frame for photographs as well.

TOGETHER WITH OUR FAMILIES

WE INVITE YOU TO CELEBRATE OUR MARRIAGE

ON SATURDAY, THE SEVENTH OF OCTOBER

TWO THOUSAND TEN

AT THREE O'CLOCK IN THE AFTERNOON

OUR LADY OF LOURDES CHURCH . NEW YORK CITY

RECEPTION IMMEDIATELY FOLLOWING

NEW YORK BOTANICAL GARDEN

NEW YORK CITY

MARIANNA MARCELA CRUZ

DAVID KEITH HARDING

Hannah and Joshua Case
20 Sutton Place South
York, New York
10022

THIS PAGE I wanted this petite nosegay of *Nigella* and scented lemon geranium to feel a bit precious, so I wrapped the bouquet in this Japanese vine, letting it trail down in several long loops. The small, lanternlike peas hanging from the vine feel like elegant charms tangled in and around the flowers.

OPPOSITE The laser-cut branch seems to reach out and grow across this invitation, designed by Modern Press Stationery. The white-colored card is backed with green paper, giving life to the cutout. This summons is delivered in a box, adding a special quality to the moment when it arrives.

RIGHT The beautiful and bold centerpiece is clearly the star of this table, but look closely and you'll find that even the smallest of details contributes to the chic and effortless look. I used a crisp white tablecloth to set the stage and then turned my attention to the centerpiece. I wanted it to feel organic and luxurious but not at all fussy. This vintage punchbowl from the 1930s was a great find. It has a unique iridescent milk glass quality to it that makes it extra-special. I love taking an object like this and giving it a whole new life. To begin, I created a layer of green hellebores for these exquisite orchids to rest on. Notice how both the flower and foliage of the hellebore are the exact some color; it's so intriguing, as if nature made a beautiful mistake.

Next came the white *Phalaenopsis* orchids; they feel as if they are literally dripping down over the top of the hellebores. These exotic blooms are about as chic as it gets, which, unfortunately, is reflected in their price. Tightly clustered white dogwood would be a lovely, much less expensive option. Tucked in and around the two flowers you'll find a few leafy ferns for texture and interest.

In lieu of a charger plate, I folded these oversized green napkins from Napa into large squares and then laid a small spray of hellebore on top. The monochromatic effect is quite chic. I was not only drawn to the color of these napkins, but to the decorative stitching around the edge as well; the embellishment reminded me of the viny motif on our inspirational bead.

I love how unexpected a colored glass can feel at a formal event. If you have a really tight palette, like we do, consider using a special glass like the green one I chose here. Not only is the color spot-on, the shape is organic and beautiful. They are hand-blown, making each glass unique.

I found these white ceramic votives that feature a sweet stitching detail that lets the warm candlelight peak through. Their design relates nicely to my Portuguese bead. To finish things off, I brought in white bentwood chairs—their clean, curved shape adds a nice bit of character to this table.

Menu

CHILLED MAINE LOBSTER SALAD TOWER
PETITE GREENS, MANGO, DICED CUCUMBER
AND LATE SUMMER HARVEST TOMATOES
CUCUMBER MELON GAZPACHO EMULSION

ROASTED TOURNEDOS OF DRY AGED ANGUS BEEF
FOIE GRAS SAUCE
LOCAL SWEET POTATOES, CHANTERELLE MUSHROOMS
AND PETALS OF BRUSSEL SPROUTS

PETITE WEDDING CAKES
BY SYLVIA WEINSTOCK

LEFT If you want a really fragrant bouquet, one that will make you smile every time you catch a sweet whiff, then consider lily of the valley as your star flower. It smells amazing, and is a classic choice for weddings. The tiny bell shape is so dear. Working my way out, I started with a large bunch of lily of the valley and then ringed the bouquet with some snowdrops. I'm obsessed with the combination of these two blooms—the lily of the valley is delicate and sweet, while the snowdrops, with their green-tipped petals, seem to be an exaggerated version of the little lilies. I loosely tied off the stems with this lovely white, airy ribbon.

OPPOSITE I think it's important to let the plants do the talking—don't force a plant or flower to do something that it doesn't want to do naturally. If you keep that in mind, plants will end up doing most of the design work for you. This viny spirea cascaded beautifully down the railing and around the banister without much help from me. I tucked in some white *Dendrobium* orchids to add a touch of the exotic. It has such a lovely overgrown, English garden feeling—very classic and bridal.

LEFT Here, I show a way to turn our vintage bead into something modern and crisp. Everything, from the table and chairs to the water glasses, steers this table away from old world and directly toward modern day. I started this setting off with a large oval Saarinen table featuring that exquisite marble top for which these pieces are famous. You can rent Saarinen tables easily, but they are pricey. If your guest list is lengthy, these tables can add up. Don't worry: You can start with any simple round surface covered in white linen and you'll still end up with a modern look.

To keep the arrangements simple and modern I left out the flowers and worked with some grassy green foliage instead.

These faceted ceramic pots echo the shape of the bead beautifully while providing a base for our almost hedgelike arrangements. It's dynamic when something feels modern and rustic all at the same time.

To bring in more of this fantastic green color, I used large green pillar candles and sat them atop oval white trays to catch the wax. I dotted simple white glass votives all around the table for some extra added glow.

I continued the modern vibe with stemless glasses filled with lime-infused water and then used simple modern plates topped with white napkins that I wrapped in climbing fig vines to finish each individual setting.

These oval-backed ghost chairs echo the shape of the Saarinen table beautifully. Ghost chairs are modern and fresh. I like how they basically disappear yet still make a huge design statement.

THOUGHTS ON USING BRANCHES

- Branches are great for building tall arrangements. Always chic and elegant, they have natural height, allowing you to avoid the traditional, cliché, or standard approach when florists try to force flowers to be tall.
- Branches instantly give structure to a bouquet without a lot of fuss. They lend a more ethereal feel by creating loose lines that cascade beautifully. They also help to achieve an organic quality that can be tough to attain when piecing together a bouquet.
- If you're using branches with blossoms, it's nice to just let the branches do their thing and not busy them up with more flowers.
- Make sure you follow the lines of the branches, as opposed to forcing them to do something different—that negates the whole point of using them in the first place.

LEFT This absolutely delightful take-away comes from Arak Kanofsky Studios. The idea here is that instead of giving a "favor," you're bestowing a "token of affection" on each of your guests. The designers did a beautiful job of interpreting my Portuguese bead.

What's inside: Notice that the shape of the butter cookie is exactly like that of the bead. The hand-painted (or iced, if you will) vine motif comes directly from the botanical artwork on the bead. The designers incorporated the couple's now mutual last initial into the design to further personalize the gift. Instead of simply stacking a bunch of cookies inside this tube, each treat gets strung along some rustic rope, separated by a round lacquered bead. Not only does the bead pay homage to our inspiration, it creates an exaggerated play on those old candy necklaces from our childhoods as well. The tube itself is decorated with a printed pattern the designers created, also based on the bead. Though the bead is mine, they took the design one step further and created a little label telling the story of how our imaginary couple came across their inspirational object. I love how they thought of everything!

OPPOSITE This vintage Haeger vase was a great find—the rich green hue and old-world feel fit perfectly with our Portuguese inspiration. The vessel's height allowed me to work with some tall and woody hydrangeas, giving the whole arrangement some real presence. A display of this size is meant to greet your guests as they arrive at your ceremony or reception. Remember how easy it is to switch things around, so consider using it for both.

LEFT, FOLLOWING PAGE This table feels organic and effortless—it's completely intoxicating. I can just imagine a group of longtime friends sitting here for hours, reliving wonderful old memories into the wee hours of the morning.

For a twist on the typical soup or salad first-course option, Marcey Brownstein Catering & Events came up with a delicious version of both for everyone to share. The idea here is that the soup and salad get laid down at alternating place settings, so that on either side of you, you'll find a friend willing to swap your spoonful of soup for a bite of their salad.

To create this rustic look, I worked with a stunning farm table that deserves to be seen. I wouldn't be able to bring myself to cover up this beautiful wood with a cloth even if I'd planned to. Instead of using fabric or even paper as a table runner, I created three elongated arrangements to do the job instead. Remember those black-and-white-patterned vessels I showed you back in our inspirational objects picture? I love the contrast they create here with this earthy table. In an effort to develop that runnerlike feel, I used trailing passion vine and exotic *Phalaenopsis* orchids. The arrangements feel as if they're reaching down the table for one another.

To keep that organic and earthy feeling going, I chose irregularly shaped plates that had a nice handmade quality to them. These stamped napkins, also featured amongst our inspirational pieces, did all the decorating for me; they help each place setting remain uncluttered, as they need no further embellishment.

My first instinct was to work with the benches that belonged with this table, but as things started to come together, I pulled in these white bentwood chairs instead. I like the contrast between the organic quality of the table and the clean lines of chairs; the combination feels unpredictable in a lovely way.

THIS PAGE, OPPOSITE This sunchoke, ramp, and nettle soup can be served chilled or warm. The bright, verdant green of this purée contrasts beautifully against the crème fraîche garnish and the white bowl. Whimsical fiddlehead ferns and green- and white-tipped asparagus add a nice seasonal touch.

THIS PAGE This arrangement has an awesome, crazy, exotic-meets-traditional feeling. I like bringing together these two worlds in unexpected ways. I decided to work with living plants rather than cut flowers to create this lush botanical arrangement made entirely out of greenery and foliage.

THIS PAGE   I love how exotic this garden bouquet feels. I wanted to focus on using the color green alone to invoke the rich botanical vibe of the bead. I kept layering *Scabiosa*, *Dianthus*, hellebores, *Hypericum* berries, bunny tail grasses, and different ferns to achieve the oval shape and lush look that I'd envisioned.

THOUGHTS ON USING WREATHS

- You could hang a wreath at the entrance to your ceremony location, creating a warm welcome that lets your guests know just where to go.
- If you're getting married in front of a beautiful old tree, consider hanging a wreath to help define your outdoor altar.
- Consider tying a wreath to the end of each pew or bench at your place of worship.
- You could reserve seats for your most special guests by hanging petite wreaths from the backs of their chairs.
- Loop a ribbon through a wreath and have your flower girl carry it down the aisle for a sweet alternative to a basket of flower petals.
- Wreaths could make a simple and elegant low centerpiece. Place them artfully along a table and sprinkle some votives around for warmth.
- Definitely consider reusing your wreaths; they couldn't be an easier element to repurpose—simply take them down and hang them back up just about anywhere.

LEFT White-glazed ceramic pots filled with oregano, sage, peppermint, parsley, and spearmint serve two purposes here. Not only are they a charming and useful favor for guests to bring home at the end of the evening, they bring life to an escort card table as well. Propped up against each pot, guests will find their names and table assignments on little cards baring the same botanical motif as our invitation. This idea could work with any little plant, but just remember, to keep things looking neat and fresh, cover the exposed soil with moss.

OPPOSITE Wreaths are a wonderful multipurpose decoration; their possible uses are endless. I worked with green hellebores, white *Nerines*, and several fern varieties, including maidenhair, to create this lush example. As a finishing touch I wrapped the base of the wreath in *Smilax*, giving it an added layer of visual interest and depth.

SCHOOLHOUSE MAP

Why a Schoolhouse Map?

When I was an art student in San Francisco, nearly every penny I had went into my art; I was always searching for cool objects to inspire me. Inside one of my favorite shops, I discovered these large schoolhouse maps, and, though I couldn't afford them at the time, I knew I had to have them. I decided to offer the friendly shop owner some of my artwork as a trade for the maps and, to my absolute delight, she agreed. I've kept them stored away forever, knowing that some day I would pull them out for something really special.

Maps instantly conjure up thoughts of travel, enticing us with all the wonderful destinations the world has to offer. I enjoy staring at them, tracing my finger from here to there, wondering when I'll have the opportunity to explore all the places I long to visit. The idea of a treasure map intrigues me as well—it holds the possibility that something wonderful is out there waiting for you, if only you can locate the big X that marks the spot. I tapped into this inspiration by featuring lots of silvery and glinting pieces that feel as if they might have just been discovered inside some sunken, newly salvaged treasure chest.

What About the Palette?

I love the colors used in these fantastic old maps: the pale pinks, creams, greens, and yellows, and those wide expanses of watery blue that come together to create this beautiful, vintage palette. The graphic black detailing is inspiring as well.

Who Is the Client?

This inspiration is perfect for the couple that loves classic details, but wants to avoid a stuffy, formal event. I can't help but imagine a bride who wants to accommodate her mother's wish to host the event at the local yacht club, yet is trying to infuse the space with her own sense of romance and effortless style.

Where and When?

A slightly more Victorian venue would be lovely with an inspiration like this, maybe the local country club, or perhaps the nearest botanical garden. I can also picture a map-infused wedding in an elegant white tent by the water, be it at a beach, a river, or a beautiful lake. I definitely envision an event like this taking place in spring or summer.

My Focus

I'm drawn to how old world and rustic and yet chic and modern maps can be. I show here how to incorporate all of these styles. You can blend romantic décor classics, like vintage silver and cherry blossoms, with a more casual, contemporary aesthetic, ending up with the best of both worlds.

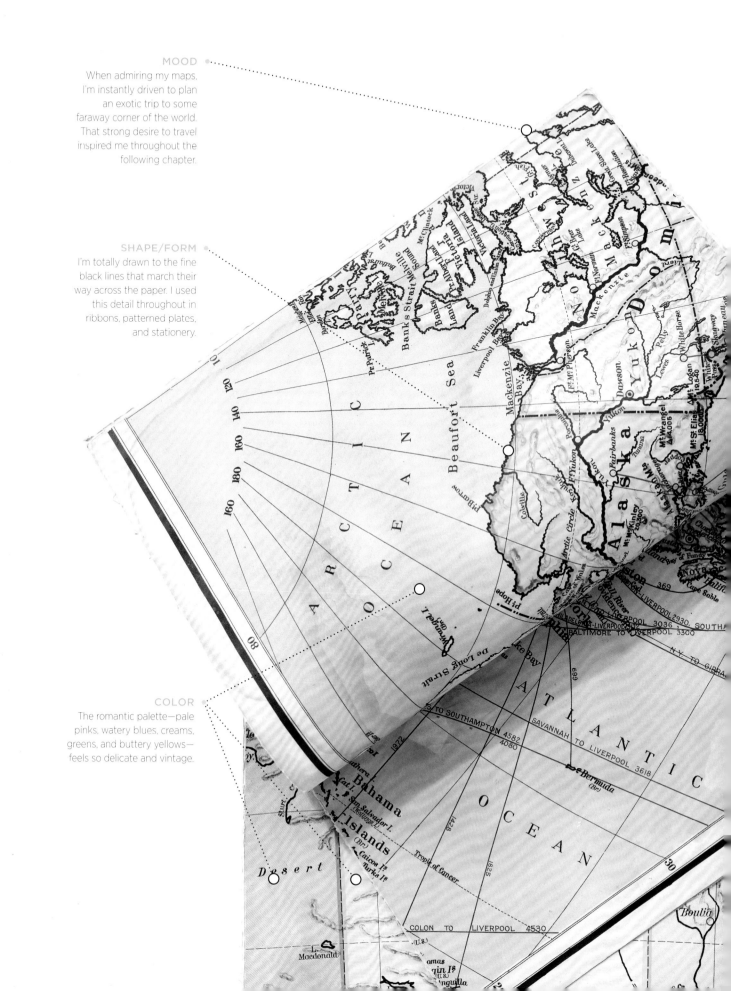

MOOD

When admiring my maps, I'm instantly driven to plan an exotic trip to some faraway corner of the world. That strong desire to travel inspired me throughout the following chapter.

SHAPE/FORM

I'm totally drawn to the fine black lines that march their way across the paper. I used this detail throughout in ribbons, patterned plates, and stationery.

COLOR

The romantic palette—pale pinks, watery blues, creams, greens, and buttery yellows—feels so delicate and vintage.

HUNTED AND GATHERED

OPPOSITE There is something wonderful about staring at a map; you instantly begin to dream up luxurious trips to far-away destinations. And who doesn't want to come upon a lost treasure map leading to some special discovery? I set about finding those shiny, glinting pieces that would look right at home in a sunken treasure chest.

CUSTARD CUPS—The color of these little aqua and green custard cups fits right in with our map motif.

ITALIAN COTTON RIBBON—This gorgeous black ribbon is a wonderful nod to the demarcation lines that march across my vintage maps.

SILVER BUD VASES—As long as the flowers have thin stems, you can make a lovely arrangement inside a single bud vase.

CERAMIC VASE—I love the cool aqua blue of this vase.

SMALL SILVER COMPOTE—Wouldn't this make for an adorable sugar bowl?

GLITTERED TABLE NUMBER—The tarnished old-world vibe is perfect for a map inspired table setting.

VINTAGE POSTCARD—Conjures up memories of travel and adventures abroad!

SILVER BASKET—Reminiscent of the latitude and longitude lines on our schoolhouse map.

ENAMELED PAIL—The perfect container for collecting sea glass on the beach.

PISTACHIO CAKE—The pistachios give this cake the ideal green tone—and it's delicious too.

SILVER TEA BOX—I always keep cuttings and swatches from my favorite ribbons in tins like this.

LEFT Here I show how our gathering of objects transitions beautifully into a vintage map–inspired table setting. Look closely and you'll be hard pressed to find a single piece missing.

To begin, I laid down a watery blue tablecloth to set the mood and then layered a runner of parchment-colored linen on top to help anchor our floral arrangements. Mixing the colored ceramic pieces with the shiny vintage silver ones allows the map palette to shine through. These colored vases are perfect for making flowers pop. I chose the aqua blue piece to set off the pink garden roses, sweet pea, and plum-colored *Fritillaria* in a way that white never could. And I tucked those apricot-colored *Ranunculus* into that mint green vessel because the colors look amazing against one another. The chartreuse vase helps these yellow tulips, *Fritillaria*, and geraniums to stand out, while the small arrangement of hyacinths looks lovely in that green glass custard cup. Remember those silver bud vases? Well, instead of taking them literally and placing a single blossom inside each one, I nestled in an entire arrangement of anemones, sweet pea, and jasmine, creating an interesting juxtaposition.

These Limoges plates offer up the graphic black detailing that is present on our maps. I topped them each with a crisp linen napkin, wrapped in black cotton ribbon.

Using trays to create groupings is one of my favorite techniques; I love vignettes within vignettes. These vintage silver pieces worked their way in seamlessly. I sprinkled mercury glass votives throughout to up the glamour quotient even more. And notice the number of small satellite moments tucked in to catch your eye; they make the whole table feel more decadent.

If you are going to use ribbons, don't go out and buy
a hundred yards of one particular double-faced satin. Mix it up
while staying within your palette. Here I brought together a
wide range of ribbons, all from Tinsel Trading, making it easy to
choose the right one for each task.

THIS PAGE This tailored garden bouquet has a modern feel. With its buttery garden roses, chartreuse zinnias, blue *Tweedia*, lilac *Scabiosa*, and touches of pink *Gomphrena* and sweet pea, the palette is fresh yet wonderfully vintage. Surrounding this beautiful array is flowering andromeda, for a little added texture.

TOP LEFT I collect vintage fabrics, so the choice to incorporate them into this chapter was an easy one for me. I wanted to bring some newer fabrics into the mix as well, since it's not always easy to find affordable and fitting textiles of the vintage variety. Many of these fabrics have real metal woven in, giving them a great sheen and a watery way about them. They remind me of the metallic tinge that seems to sweep over the surface of the sea once the sun has begun its evening descent. I stayed within the map palette of greens, blues, silver, and gold to make sure that everything took on a very cohesive feel. The striped one is my favorite! Textiles like these from Tinsel Trading in Manhattan would be great for making table runners or overlays, but could be used for any decorative accent.

BOTTOM LEFT I've noticed that old maps usually have some sort of interesting finishing edge to them, so I went in search of some trimmings that invoked the same emotions in me that the maps do. While poking around in Tinsel Trading, I came across a wide variety of ropes, ribbons, and cording that fit the bill perfectly. Of course many maps have a nautical vibe, making it easy to pull in yachting and sailing influences, so I was naturally drawn to these striped and aqua ropes. The lacy ribbons work well with the map palette and they add some wonderful textures to the mix. Trims like this are great for tying off your bouquet, or perhaps for lining a table runner. The cording could be used to delineate a reserved row at your ceremony as well. The possibilities are endless.

OPPOSITE This lovely bouquet makes me think of Audrey Hepburn. It's a petite tailored nosegay fashioned from pink and green *Ranunculus*, with some added gray foliage for texture and interest—the foliage also keeps it from becoming too sweet. The floral colors, once again, echo the wonderful palette of our inspirational vintage map, as does the watery aqua of the vintage silk ribbon used to tie off the handle. I couldn't resist featuring the bouquet inside of this lovely silver compote. When I happened upon it, I felt as if I had discovered something that was recovered from a treasure chest, salvaged from the depths of the sea. It has such an old-world, exotic feel.

THOUGHTS ON SETTING THE TABLE

- As you dream up your table setting, it's very important to remember that everything needs space, as well as some surrounding room to breathe. If you're going to have lots of elements, like large and small floral arrangements, bud vases, floating flowers, votives, and so on, don't forget that you have to leave room on the table for its true purpose. It may sound silly to point this out, but your guests have to eat a meal here. There must be room for plates, a few pieces of stemware, flatware, seating cards, and napkins. You don't want to spend time and money creating this stunning table setting, only to realize that it is too crowded to work.
- Take into account the size and shape of your table as well as how many guests will be sitting there. The more guests, the more crowded it will become. Creating an intimate feeling is great, but it's definitely not achieved by forcing your friends and family to sit just inches from one another.
- Whenever you find a beautiful table that doesn't need to be covered up, by all means, let its natural beauty shine.
- If you love the old-world elegance of tall arrangements and want to feature them at your reception, I definitely recommend building them with branches. Always chic and elegant, branches are naturally tall, so they help you avoid what I call the "lollipop" arrangement. You know, the ones where the flowers form a poof on top and the vase just sticking out from the bottom.
- Remember that a table can look naked if decorated exclusively with tall arrangements, so add in some medium-sized and smaller pieces that help draw the eye back down to conversation level.

LEFT Here I dressed up a rented wooden farm table with a simple blue burlap runner. I anchored both ends of the table with these large branch arrangements made entirely out of white cherry blossoms. Then, to marry the tall elements with what's happening down below, I mixed in some smaller vases containing cherry blossoms and pale pink *Ranunculus*. I added yet another layer by floating creamy peonies in silver bowls. Separately, each piece is lovely, but by combining them together in one setting, you give the eye somewhere beautiful to travel. Lastly, I sprinkled in some mercury glass votives, giving everything a dreamy quality. I think what makes this setting special is the mix of elegant silver pieces with the wooden table.

THIS PAGE Gifts for the Good Life used the graphic map imagery to create these fantastic little tokens. *Welcome:* Upon arrival at their room, a lovely door tag greets your guests. *Farewell:* The night before departure, have these luggage tags printed with your guest's return address, left in their rooms.

OPPOSITE I love how fresh this hand-tied bouquet feels. Notice how the tiny blue *Tweedia* blooms echo the shape of the larger white anemones. Pairing flowers that share a quality yet are different will give you a textured look. The contrast of the softer lilac adds even more visual interest.

WELCOME

FAREWELL
safe and happy travels!
Mr. and Mrs. Michael Davenport
36 Finley Street, Apartment 2B
Boston, Massachusetts 02116
email: davenport@yahoo.com

RIGHT Traditionally, a croquembouche is served at celebratory occasions, and since my treasured maps always bring out my desire to travel the French countryside, I couldn't resist featuring one of these towering confections. Our croquembouche from Ceci-Cela Patisserie in New York City features gold-coated almonds and caramelized sugar. I like how participatory this dessert is; everyone gets to pick a profiterole of choice and enjoy it right on the spot. To play up the French quality that I so adore, I hung one of my favorite French-feeling fabrics as a backdrop.

OPPOSITE These vases are two of my favorite containers in my rather large collection. The silver inlay artwork and the vivid blue hue live comfortably in our inspirational map world, making them a beautiful choice. I worked with a very edited palette of lilac, soft blue, cream, and dusty silver to help rein in some of that inherent wildness. I stuck with airy flowers, such as feathery astilbe, *Scabiosa*, *Tweedia*, miniature thistles, dusty miller, and *Brodiaea* to achieve this wonderfully sophisticated, blousy effect.

OPPOSITE If you choose large flowers, like these dinner plate dahlias, you only need about five of them to create a lovely and dramatic nosegay. I accented these pale pink blooms with smaller lavender blossoms, *Astrantia*, and delicate vines to complete this tailored garden bouquet. The floral palette echoes that of our inspirational maps beautifully. Sometimes when you use floppy flowers like dahlias, you need to create a collar to keep their heads perky, so I tucked in hosta leaves to provide some extra support.

ABOVE If you find yourself drawn to wild and slightly overgrown garden flowers yet naturally lean toward a more modern aesthetic, don't worry, the two can intertwine beautifully. The trick is to bring in simple, clean shapes, like these small Middle Kingdom vases, colorful glass votives, and white oval platters. The flaxseed-colored linen used here is a great neutral base—it helps give everything some air, allowing the lovely silhouettes to stand out. Let the flowers flow and do what they will; fussing over them too much interferes with the effortless modern feeling.

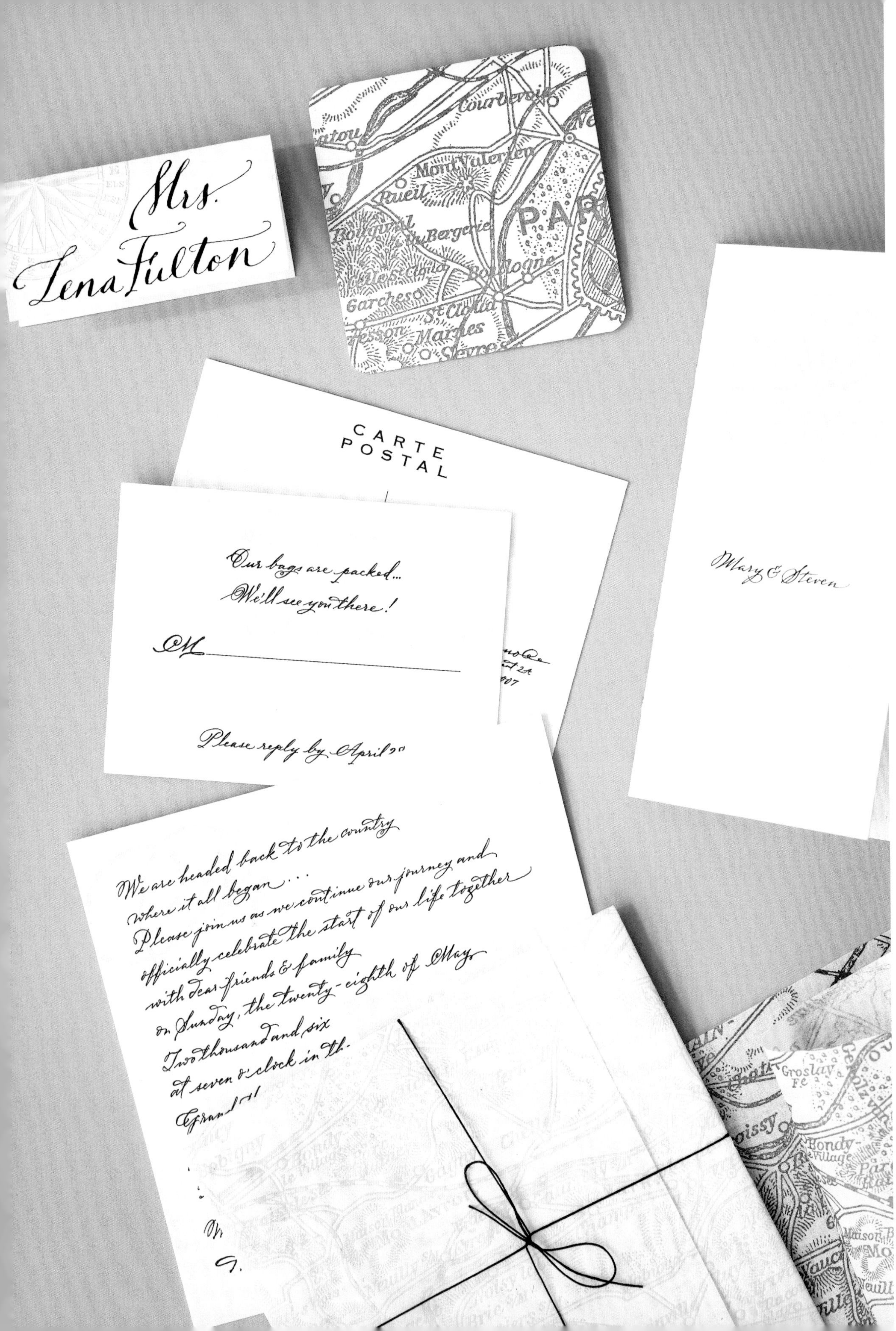

Mrs.
Lena Fulton

CARTE
POSTAL

Mary & Steven

Our bags are packed...
We'll see you there!

M_____

Please reply by April 20

We are headed back to the country
where it all began . . .
Please join us as we continue our journey and
officially celebrate the start of our life together
with dear friends & family
on Sunday, the twenty-eighth of May
Two thousand and six
at seven o'clock in the
Grand H

OPPOSITE One of my favorite things about this map-inspired stationery is how it can be personalized to the couple. Did you share your first kiss on the streets of San Francisco, or cement your love on holiday in San Tropez? Well, find a fantastic vintage or even modern map of your special place and feature it in the wedding stationery. As this suite of stationery by Modern Press was designed to coordinate with my vintage maps, the style takes on a decidedly more antique feel. The fine black script of this lovely calligraphy relates nicely to the delineation lines scrawled all across the maps, as does the old-world feel of this style of writing.

ABOVE As a general rule, your wedding guests will arrive hungry; many have pared down their usual eating habits throughout the day, knowing they'll spend the night indulging. That said, by the time cocktail hour rolls around, they'll be *really* hungry. Marcey Brownstein Catering & Events came up with a lovely trio of tasting plates to keep your friends and family satisfied.

Clockwise from lower left: Grilled peach salad with frisée, bacon, and pistachios, paired with a white peach and basil martini; salmon with tomato, mint, and green onion salsa, paired with a mint Mojito; squid-ink linguini with shrimp, fennel, artichoke, and blackberry reduction served with sparkling wine accented with a blackberry.

THOUGHTS ON BOUQUETS
BRIDAL BOUQUETS

- I like to leave stems showing when I finish a bouquet—it's much more natural looking.
- Most people tend not to think of branches as a viable option for a bouquet, but I view them as a stand-out choice. They instantly give you structure without a lot of fussing around, and they achieve an organic quality that can be difficult to get when piecing together a bouquet.
- I don't like it when the bride's bouquet is just a larger version of the bridesmaids'. The bride's bouquet should be something beautiful and unique, featuring superspecial flowers.
- Consider using metallic ribbons on your bridal bouquet; the glamour will help set your bouquet apart.

BRIDESMAIDS' BOUQUETS

- Keeping your bridesmaids' bouquets small allows them to be lush without being too pricey.
- I try to choose flowers that have interesting and different textures so that each bridesmaid receives something totally unique. If you put roses in one bouquet and peonies in another, the difference, in the end, won't make a difference.
- If the bride is using a variety of flowers in her own bouquet, I think it's a great idea to stick to one type of blossom for each of the bridesmaids. It's a nice way to make them all feel special! The same goes for color—if the bride has a mixture within her own bouquet, feature a single color with each bridesmaid's arrangement.

LEFT This dreamy sea blue, tufted couch immediately made me think of my maps. The "wateriness" of it couldn't be more ideal, and the classic vintage shape fits in perfectly. I imagine it might once have had a home in Argentina or Spain. Resting atop this lovely sofa is a beautiful bouquet featuring cherry blossom branches and sweat pea, a combination I love together. I added in some alligator fern foliage too, as a nod to our exotic travel theme. To finish things off, I went with an extrawide, aqua green satin ribbon.

LEFT Again, I created a variety of boutonnieres for the guys to choose from. I think it's nice to keep boutonnieres on the smaller, textural side, versus making them big and fluffy: You're not trying to emasculate the men, after all. To the left we have *Veronica* with oregano and lavender. In the middle you'll find *Astrantia*, a *Scabiosa* pod, and oregano. And to the right I've featured sweet pea and *Tweedia*. Each boutonniere is finished with a wrapping of rustic twine.

OPPOSITE I'm obsessed with how yummy and lush and abundant this cascading bouquet feels! The jasmine and superlong flowering oregano accent the more dominant hydrangea exquisitely. A showstopper like this is perfect for a bride with a simple, elegant dress—the bouquet and dress shouldn't fight for attention. If you want a hydrangea-heavy bouquet like this, talk to your florist about using more delicate varieties with soft and curvy stems. These tend to be locally grown and available in seasonal varieties. Be sure to vary the colors as well; this classic bouquet transitions from purple to lilac to pink absolutely beautifully.

THOUGHTS ON A BUBBLY BAR

- A bubbly bar is a great alternative to serving a signature cocktail at your wedding or event.
- Such a bar gives your guests another destination to visit within your reception or cocktail hour.
- This bar is a great way to pump up the traditional bar, while making it slightly interactive.
- Play with different types of stemware, and pair different options with each variety of sparkling wine.
- You can let guests further customize their choices by having fresh berries nearby that can be dropped into their champagne. If your event takes place during the day, consider offering fresh-squeezed orange juice for Mimosas.
- Make sure you mix it up by providing a selection of Prosecco, sparkling wines, and Champagnes. Most venues and caterers will have their standard offerings, but feel free to supplement with things you love. You can always source your own alcohol, and sometimes your caterer will ask if you want to take on this part of the planning, enabling you to pick out exactly what you want. Either way, make sure you have a variety of bubblies to choose from.
- Have fun using different styles of ice and champagne buckets to keep things cool. Ask your caterer and rental company to see what they have to offer.
- If you're having a beach or backyard wedding, consider using enamel buckets for a more laid-back and fun look.
- Choose a bar-height table for this display; it helps it to feel more chic and special.
- If you decide to feature a bubbly bar during your cocktail hour, have some little snacks nearby, perhaps even ones that pair well with each vintage.

RIGHT At the base of our bubbly bar, I placed a luxurious metallic gray fabric. I chose these silver ice buckets to house our bubblies because they have this wonderful, old-world feel that reminded me of traveling on a luxury yacht. I gave each variety its own style of stemware just for fun. I added another layer of visual interest by sectioning off each vintage with a thin ribbon: The black line running down the center of this ribbon makes me think of all the demarcation lines running across our inspirational maps. To complete the table, Marcey Brownstein Catering & Events created some delicate little nibbles, like petite deviled eggs with radicchio-infused sea salt, delicious radishes with gray sea salt, and *far-far* crackers in various pink tones. I played with using different silver trays to display all of these snacks.

TWINE

Why This Twine?

I'm always on the prowl for little decorative touches; every shop I walk by has the potential to produce some fancy little ribbon or trim for my collection. Hardly a day goes by when I'm not wrapping something, be it a gift or the stems of some flowery bouquet. So when I see something unique like this French twine, I buy it immediately, knowing that someday it will come in handy. When planning an event, it's important to keep your eyes peeled for any little thing that might spark a design idea; you never know where your greatest inspiration might come from.

What About the Palette?

I was drawn to the rich fall color palette of this twine. People often assume that pumpkin orange must be present in one form or another to do this season justice, but this warm ocher yellow, paired with olive green, and bookended by crimson red is a wonderful tribute to autumn. The colors really evoke early fall, when the leaves have just begun to change—some have turned yellow and red while others are still holding on to their green, though that green has long ago lost its summer vibrancy. I'm reminded of walking outdoors in the fall when the grass is still green but the leaves have created a crispy and colorful carpet to crunch your way through.

Who Is the Client?

This inspiration is perfect for the couple that wants to host a beautiful, rich autumnal event, but is looking to avoid pumpkins, gourds, and maple leaves.

Where and When?

I can picture this fall wedding in a cozy setting, perhaps a very rustic yet urban space, like the one with those beautiful exposed brick walls pictured on the following pages. These ideas would be stunning in a great barn situated somewhere out in a meadow as well. It's important that the space reflect the rich color palette and mood.

My Focus

I think most people struggle with how to bring this season to life in a chic and elegant way, so my goal is to show you how to do just that. A warm, mustard yellow like this one can often be difficult to deal with, causing people to shy away from it, especially for weddings. I think in general people like yellow tones, but don't know exactly how to use them. I wanted this chapter to give plenty of ideas on how to introduce this often-overlooked color into the mix.

MOOD
There is a nice masculinity to both the palette and feel of this French twine, making it a great inspirational piece for the couple that wants to steer clear of an overly feminine vibe.

PATTERN/FORM
The ombré style of the twine creates a charming pattern repeat that I mined as inspiration for many of the fabrics and pillows I chose throughout this chapter.

COLOR
This rich autumnal palette is a wonderfully fresh take on fall; you don't have to use pumpkin orange to communicate this crisp season.

HUNTED AND GATHERED

OPPOSITE I find this color palette exciting—it's whimsical yet refined, in a French countryside sort of way. There is a nice masculinity to it. You can definitely create some wonderfully girly moments within this palette, but the gentlemen will appreciate the more gender-neutral vibe.

VINTAGE PLATE—The reddish rim and gilded edge on this plate make it special.

GLAZED BOWL—I love the mustard yellow color of this piece; it ties in perfectly with this autumnal palette.

FOLIAGE AND FLOWERS—The deep rich color of both this peony and the wonderful plum foliage become much more interesting when paired with this bright cheeky palette.

TIN—The urnlike shape of this antique Lipton tea tin is fabulous; the mottled finish adds some great texture.

POOL BALLS—I adore the shape and colors of these vintage pool balls; the dull yet shining surface is nice as well.

CRASPEDIA—Also known as billy buttons or woollyheads, these interesting yellow pom-pom–like flowers add a whimsical touch.

PRINTED FABRICS—Who doesn't love Liberty of London fabrics? Their patterns are truly one of a kind.

NAPKINS—I love the basket-weave pattern on this red-and-white napkin; it's a great update to the traditional check.

SMALL BOWL—The wonderful red color and sweet little size of this bowl drew me to it.

RIBBON—This ribbon has a nice width and charming yellow and white stripes.

RIGHT A lot of people favor fall over any other season, yet shy away from an autumn wedding or event because of the seemingly limited color palette. You don't have to plunk a bright orange jack-o'-lantern down on each table to honor this time of year; there are plenty of ways to make these colors feel sophisticated.

I chose a woven, almost rattanlike linen cloth in this warm butterscotch tone to set the stage for this twine-inspired table. Next I created arrangements featuring this striking plum foliage. Typically the lighter colors pop off the darker, but here the deep plum hue stands out against the yellow, spidery *Oncidium* orchids. The yellow, footed bowl creates another great layer of contrast against the plum. I tucked in some rosemary to add a little green. The abundant display, despite its dark color, feels airy and loose.

If you're going to feature a dark centerpiece like this, make sure the room has ample lighting. As the night wears on and your space becomes darker, the arrangement could end up looking like a dark blob on your table, so make sure to plan accordingly. In lieu of a charger, I laid down a white napkin folded into a large square. I added a sprig of rosemary at each setting as a lovely, fragrant touch. To complete the look, I accented the whole table with golden yellow votives in a variety of styles.

THOUGHTS ON CREATIVE LIGHTING
LAMP SHADES

- Consider hanging a lamp shade over each table to make your dining space feel more intimate. Even with as many as twenty or thirty tables, the effect can be stunning.
- Lamp shades are a great way to change the entire feeling of a large, high-ceilinged, stark space by visually lowering the ceiling to create a series of smaller, more intimate spaces.
- A lamp shade helps to bring your guests' focus down onto their own table.

CHANDELIERS

- Chandeliers add a touch of decadence that only a lighting fixture of such grand proportion can.
- Don't fret if your space doesn't already contain a chandelier—they are very easy to rent.
- I love hanging a few large chandeliers inside a tent; the effect is glamorous and chic.

OPPOSITE I wanted this setting to have a contemporary French cottage feel: totally chic, yet effortlessly casual. The idea is that guests will feel as if they're in your comfortable home—at a table for just a few, rather than a few hundred. I love how a lamp shade can provide that level of intimacy, which is rarely attainable in a large space. These circular white shades are beautiful, and have a stunning effect strung up above a large number of tables in an open space.

Next to the shade, the botanical-patterned tablecloth is really the star of this show; it brings our palette of yellow and deep burgundy together beautifully. The flowers featured in this wonderful cream-colored footed compote were inspired by the patterned cloth. These creamy tree peonies, with their fuzzy yellow centers and pops of deep burgundy, were the perfect choice. I added broom flowers to bring in some more yellow and a touch of green.

To keep the table from becoming too busy, I chose a simple white plate and a classic wineglass. I brought in a classic red-checked napkin to emphasis the cottagelike feeling I was aiming for, and then added in these unique votives to introduce a subtle new shape and to provide an extra little warmth as well.

THOUGHTS ON USING FURNITURE AND RUGS

- A large tree or a garden bed can help to mark out a space.
- Rugs can help to define a grouping of furniture.
- Fences are perfect for lining with furniture—they create a natural line to follow.
- Rugs are great for adding texture to the floor.
- Rugs really are best for inside spaces, but can be used in a tent as well. However, I have to admit that using one outside in the grass could create an amazingly decadent Victorian madness moment.

RIGHT Shopping for fabric can be such a wonderful source of inspiration, and a great place to begin your design process. I especially love walking away with great fabric swatches that will undoubtedly kindle new ideas in the future.

OPPOSITE This lounge space exemplifies the cool and chic autumn vibe I was going for. Nary a pumpkin in site, yet the feeling of the season shines through beautifully.

Clearly the standout piece in this lounge is this giant arrangement of plum foliage and yellow *Cymbidium* orchids. The large metal urn adds a nice rustic touch, especially when paired with the dark and moody arrangement. Big displays like this are great for defining a space; they immediately add presence.

I rented two modern couches covered in a crisp white linen and then tossed some striped pillows on top to bring in some of that vintage French country vibe that I love. I also rented this rich brown sisal rug to anchor the sofas and further define the lounge space. This table is made from reclaimed wood originally used in Chinese temples. It does a great job of showcasing how a mix of rustic and modern pieces can create an inviting space.

Atop the table, I floated peonies inside ocher and red bowls. The vessels add a wonderful pop of color, while the floating flowers are a lovely decorative touch.

It's important to keep open surfaces around for people to put down a drink or leave an empty glass behind, so make sure you keep that in mind when designing your event. And remember, a lounge area like this doesn't have to be reserved for the after-party—consider creating a similar space for your cocktail hour, giving your guests a comfortable place to catch up with friends and family right from the start.

THIS PAGE These vintage-inspired spools are a sweet, very literal translation of our twine muse. They serve as fun seating cards. Gifts for the Good Life designed them using wooden spools. They mimicked the actual twine and printed the design on paper that was then wound around each spool.

THIS PAGE This bouquet pays homage to our autumnal color palette. I didn't want to bring in a lot of foliage because often bright green takes away from rich, warm tones. I worked with burgundy astilbe, spray and garden roses in burgundy and mustard yellow, and burgundy *Scabiosa* to create this painterly bouquet.

ABOVE This simple idea is different and fun. When planning an event, most people rely on the flowers to create interest and provide color. However, here I show you how you can get both without using any floral arrangements at all. I covered the escort card table in a bold red-and-white-patterned fabric to bring in our color palette and then covered just about every inch of the surface in candles. I used tall stands with thick, squat pillars and then tucked in lots of different votives in a great variety of styles and sizes. Imagine the warm glow radiating off all of this charming silvery mercury glass!

OPPOSITE My favorite element in this bouquet is the graphic fiddlehead ferns. They have this fabulous Tim Burton–esque quality to them that's a fun nod to fall's most enchanting holiday. Along with the ferns you'll find *Celosia*, *Amaranthus*, dahlias, and some freesia, all featuring that rich autumnal palette we've been working in. I played around with layering different sizes and textures, and tried to break up the generic round shape with the pointy *Celosia* and curly ferns. Forgoing the traditional ribbon accent, I opted instead to tightly wrap the stems with some red twine; it's a great little rustic touch.

ABOVE Here I wanted to show you how a rich and moody palette can be beautiful for spring. I brought in bright green and yellow viburnum and astilbe to create these arrangements. The plum foliage adds a richness that works perfectly with these brassy gold vases. To bring the eye back down a bit, I tucked some peonies and viburnum into tea canisters. The candelabra bridges the size gap between the two floral arrangements beautifully. I softened the space by using a creamy white runner. A display like this can work well in any number of locations, from a welcome table to your seating-card table and even as your ceremony table.

THIS PAGE Here's a vibrant selection of autumnal boutonnieres. I played with materials that felt almost like fabric: The *Celosia* and *Amaranthus* both have an interesting chenillelike quality that I like. In addition, I worked with dahlias, freesia and lady's mantle, all featuring our rich color palette.

ABOVE While it was easy to see how an inspirational object like citrus fruit could be translated to the menu, other themes can be beautifully incorporated as well. The most seamless way to do so is with the color palette. Marcey Brownstein Catering & Events came up with a delicious twine-inspired trio of canapés to delight the senses.

Left to right: Heart-shaped toasted sourdough bread featuring a deconstructed beet and orange salad. Triangles of pumpernickel topped with smoked salmon, dilled crème fraîche, red onions, and fresh sage. Goat cheese, green apple, and a bit of orange zest served on brioche.

OPPOSITE This bouquet interprets our somewhat masculine color palette in a romantic and feminine way. I used two peony varieties to achieve this look: a double peony in deep burgundy and a tree peony in this wonderful creamy color featuring a vivid yellow center. I tucked in some plum foliage to add a bit of texture and subtle shine. When you're using high-contrast flowers like these for a bridal bouquet, I think it's nice to break down the palette and give each bridesmaid a single color. For this bouquet, you could have your maid of honor carry a nosegay of deep burgundy *Ranunculus*, while another bridesmaid could carry creamy garden roses.

VINTAGE TIN

Why This Vintage Tin?

This cigarette tin was a gift from Maria Vella. With the help of her niece, Maria loves to scour open-air markets and crazy antique shops while traveling. During one such shopping excursion in Turkey, she found this vintage tin and brought it back as a gift to me. I adore the exotic nature of this piece; it brings out the traveler in me. I find myself wanting to hop the next flight leaving for anywhere in the Mediterranean, to sit under a glorious palm tree upon arrival, letting the warm coastal breezes blow away my troubles. Wouldn't you just love to spend the day roaming around this castle, being treated to all its royal delights?

I've always felt that travel yields some of the best inspirational moments. When I start working with new clients, I begin by peppering them with questions about their favorite vacation spots. Have they taken any wonderful trips as a couple? Does some intimate little Parisian bistro hold a special place in their hearts? Have they brought home any interesting artwork while out seeing the world? Any and all of these details can spark a design idea that ends up shaping their whole event.

What About the Palette?

Aside from the wonderful travel theme, I'm drawn to the interesting color palette of this tin. The bright orange paired with tropical green creates an intense combination. The sandy browns in the image of the castle tweak the total effect in a unique way, while the glinting gold accents add to the overall decadence.

Who Is the Client?

The couple inspired by my tin is looking for a unique bohemian style with a decidedly luxurious overtone. They're definitely world travelers, glamorous gypsies if you will, who have cultivated a love for lush, bold details.

Where and When?

This inspiration is perfect for an urban wedding; I can see these ideas coming to life in a loft, or a wide-open, clean white space. With the venue acting as a blank canvas, luxurious details like gilded furniture, lush foliage, and sparkling stemware would become all the embellishment that you need. And what's great about an inspirational piece like this is that it really can work in any season. The metallic accents are perfect for winter, the rustic elements are great for autumn, and of course the lush greenery with orange and white accents are wonderful for spring and summer.

My Focus

I wanted to infuse everything with a slightly old-world feeling, yet keep things vibrant and interesting. The whole vibe feels luxurious, yet a bit wacky, and that wackiness is what I love most about it.

SHAPE/FORM
I was inspired by the symmetry of the palm trees, which you'll find directly reflected in one of the ceremony spaces I created for this chapter.

COLOR
The vibrant orange and fresh green make for a unique and intense palette. I love taking an unexpected color combination like this and turning it into something really beautiful.

MOOD
Once again, travel becomes the driving force behind my inspiration. It's so easy for my mind to get swept away to this Mediterranean castle.

PRINCE DE MONACO

ED. LAURENS

HUNTED AND GATHERED

OPPOSITE Inspired by the crazy nature of this tin, I brought in some glinting metallic gold finishes, interesting foliage, and bright colors. The combination of these pieces together feels decadent and wonderfully exotic.

VINTAGE GOLD FLOWERS—Each petal is actually an individual ashtray, but despite their less-than-romantic purpose, the gold finish and floral shape make them one of my favorites.

GOLD TROPHY—I love small vases such as this trophy.

METAL BASKETS—The open work and decorative roping on these baskets caught my eye; the off-white and bronze finishes are great too.

FOLIAGE—These crazy, exotic leaves and little bits of wonderful foliage remind me of palm trees.

LINENS—Orange and gold linens are a simple way to incorporate the palette.

DRINKING GLASS—The gold base on this lovely glass makes it special.

WHITE CERAMIC PINEAPPLE—These make wonderful objects for your tin-inspired table.

WHITE PITCHER—The gold rim on this pitcher gives it that little extra something that I love.

SUCCULENTS—Succulents make me think of dry, desertlike places, which I happen to find really beautiful. The subtle green of these plants is wonderful with this palette.

RIGHT This setting is all about drawing on the exotic and rustic vibe of far-away Morocco. I played up those two wonderful traits in an interesting way.

I chose creamy white linens for both the tablecloth and napkins, as pure white could have worked against the rustic feeling we're going for. These old olive oil urns do a great job of emphasizing our rustic influences; I gave each one a modern tweak by filling it with just a single style of flower. The two on the left contain different varieties of *Asclepia*, while the third holds these spindly orange thistles.

I find that trays can be a useful addition to any tabletop décor. Here I used some copper serving pieces to create a mock runner down the center of the table. I placed two of the urns on top and then filled in with some oranges and beautiful Moroccan tea glass votives. To bring your eye out from the larger jugs, I dotted a few single dahlias around the table, nestled inside little coppery cups.

Each place setting features ornate silver flatware, a white plate rimmed with gold (as a nod to the gold touches on our tin), and the creamy white soft napkin. For another moment of color, I placed a single orange calla lily at each seat.

OPPOSITE Though there must be thousands and thousands of floral varieties in the world, people often think of roses before any other blooms. They have a sense of tradition about them, an old-world quality that's hard to deny. I wanted to embrace that feeling, but with a tweak of course. I love how wacky and almost out of place these tropical leaves look when paired with pale orange and yellow roses; they add a really interesting exotic flair to this very classic flower.

ABOVE A really free and fresh arrangement like this one anchoring our altar is best used indoors. If you placed something like this outside in a garden or a rolling meadow, it would most certainly get lost. However, against a beautiful plaster wall, inside a great barn, or even in an urban loft, this effortless display of echinacea, butterfly bush, cosmos, and various fragrant herbs like thyme catches the eye. I love using a botanical-patterned rug like this in lieu of the traditional white aisle runner.

ABOVE This whole scene looks as if it might have taken place in Cuba back in the twenties. I wanted this idea to remain classic, yet have an exotic, faraway feel. With the bouquet, my focus was to play up these white-and-cream-colored roses, and then accent them with just a little bit of orange, which I did by tucking in some *Asclepia*. These interesting tropical leaves create the perfect frame for the more traditional flowers. To finish things off, I used a superwide vintage ribbon around the stems.

OPPOSITE In my opinion, if you're going to build something exotic and a bit crazy like this arrangement, it's best to use a vessel similar to the gold one I've chosen here. A piece like this adds some glamour to all this wackiness. This arrangement is filled with lots of different forms of foliage, and just a few flowers. I wanted the flowers to accent the foliage, rather than the other way around. Inside you'll find lady's mantle, dracaena leaves, and passion vine, with just a touch of orchids and a few parrot tulips. For a little something extra and fun, I tucked in some baby pineapples to really play up the exotic vibe.

ABOVE My vintage tin has always conjured up thoughts of traveling through exotic locations rich with art, history, and inspiration. I wanted to honor that inspiration by creating a family-style feast of tagine pots filled with authentic Moroccan flavors. Not only do the tagines hold a delicious dinner inside; they become beautiful table decorations as well. This visually stunning variation by Marcey Brownstein Catering & Events features tomatoes, zucchini, onions, and carrots served with a sweet pea and lemon zest orzo salad. Tagine stews can be vegetarian or feature seafood or meat, so have your caterer create several options for each table, ensuring the satisfaction of all your guests.

OPPOSITE This ceremony design is a great example of taking a stark and empty urban space and making it feel more lush and inviting. I love the way the two palm trees become the frame for the scene on the tin, so I wanted to re-create that in this ceremony space. The palms anchor the end of the aisle, creating a frame in which vows will be said. To dress up the trees a bit, I planted ferns and little orange accent flowers around the bases of the trees. Trailing down the aisle are a few rented ferns sitting on copper trays. I clustered some citrus fruits around each pot to bring some of that great color down to the ground. These white chairs add a great modern touch to this setting; I like how airy they make the space.

RENTING PLANTS

- Consider approaching your local family-owned nursery about renting plants, shrubs, and trees. Offer to pay them half the purchase price to rent them for one day. You can definitely try to strike a bargain, as it's really in their favor to make a deal.
- Rented trees can help bring texture to any space. Take a survey of your indoor location and then decide which areas would benefit from their height and lushness.
- Most likely you'll have to buy many plants that, for some reason, don't survive the festivities, but it's still a better deal than purchasing them all and then having to figure out what to do with them after the event.

RIGHT This table setting is a more modern reflection of our vintage tin inspiration and has a great graphic and fresh feeling. Instead of your average white tablecloth, I laid down this deep orange cloth to create a vibrant canvas on which to work. I'm a big fan of using color in this way. The white circular plates contrast starkly against this cloth and the white votives echo the shapes and crispness all around the table.

The napkins, featuring a slightly paler shade of orange, are tied into little bundles with white ribbon; each bow incorporates a mini hosta leaf for color and fun. I kept things modern with stainless steel flatware and stemless wine- and water glasses. The repeating round shapes create a lot of visual interest. The wild centerpiece is a mixture of succulents and dracaena leaves and plants, with a few red *Gloriosa* flowers tucked in for color.

ABOVE Here is a superclean yet exotic ceremony space—it's one of my favorites. It's fairly easy to accomplish as long as you have the means with which to reach the ceiling. I created these lush, tropical garlands by entwining white *Phalaenopsis* orchids with olive branches. I tucked in some deep orangey-red viburnum to add a touch of color. If you're featuring a lot of white like this, it's nice to have a painted wall or colored curtain as your backdrop; it helps the white to pop. For an outdoor ceremony, consider wrapping two sturdy poles with a garland just like this; the effect will be slightly different, but the garland will appear just as fresh and lovely.

OPPOSITE This cascading bouquet is stunning. I adore how drapey and loose it feels. The flowers are so delicate some of them look almost like thin paper. Most people wouldn't think to put orchids and tulips together, but parrot tulips have a wonderfully exotic feel to them that pairs well with the more unusual orchids—I like the strangeness of the combination. In addition, I used calla lilies, *Gloriosa*, and trailing passion vine to achieve this look.

THIS PAGE I like taking a clean, modern vase in a very organic shape and pairing it with lush and crazy flowers. I worked with parrot tulips, garden roses, lady's mantle, and a few wild grasses to create this lush arrangement. A mixture of fruit and flowers can be beautiful. For a pop of color, I tucked in jewel-like pomegranates.

RIGHT I often present my clients with a box of assorted boutonnieres; it allows the groom to choose something that he likes, since, let's be honest here, he may be not making all that many choices throughout this process. The rest of the guys in the wedding party can choose too, which they'll appreciate, even if they don't mention it. As long as they are within the palette, it's not necessary for all the boutonnieres to match—I think it's way more fun if they don't.

From the top down: A yellow garden rose paired with a green hellebore. A rich, rusty-colored calla lily with some passion vine leaves. An orange orchid with a few dracaena leaves. An almost blood orange–toned orchid with a coleus leaf. Each boutonniere is finished with a little bit of ribbon in a complementary style.

LEFT This table setting evokes a treasure trove of fabulous travel souvenirs from a few shopping adventures in Morocco or maybe Greece. I adore how rich and colorful it is—the palette is very precise, making it quite clean looking despite the jumble of objects and flowers. Our vintage tin inspiration comes through loud and clear in everything from the colors to the exotic foliage, the gold accents, and the unique pineapples.

To start, I covered the table with a crisp white cloth and then laid down an interesting white-and-taupe-patterned runner from which to build the décor. The subtle pattern adds a wonderful layer of visual interest to the finished table.

I laid down square plates and then folded white napkins to fit perfectly inside the rims. Each napkin was then adorned with a gorgeous bright orange orchid. The bright silver flatware helps the whole table feel elegant, while the slightly more modern stemware adds a nice touch.

I brought together a wide variety of pitchers, vases, and bowls to hold a number of beautiful floral arrangements. Because there are so many different things happening on this table, I decided not to mix the flowers up and allowed each variety to shine on its own. The unique red pitcher holds soft and fluttery white sweet pea blossoms, accented with some exotic citron-colored leaves; the clean white vase contains striking orangey-red calla lilies; and the brown-footed urn holds more white sweet pea, this time paired with another variety of exotic foliage that has a wonderful striping detail to it. Finally, the white, orange-banded pitcher contains crazy and fun bright orange parrot tulips. The foliage in each arrangement gives the flowers a base from which to really pop.

Mixing objects into your table setting is a great way to create an interesting, eclectic look. The pineapples work perfectly with our vintage tin–inspired table. However, you might also consider things like books and clocks as an alternative. The orange-yellow votive holders add another punch of color and give a lovely warm glow as night edges out the day.

ENGLISH PITCHER

Why This English Pitcher?

My first professional love will always be flowers, so it's not hard to see why I'm attracted to a pitcher like this. Not only does the beautiful, painterly floral motif draw us in, but I can't help starting to imagine the arrangement I would build to tuck inside. To me, every vessel I see falls into two categories: Either I can put flowers into it, or I cannot. Typically, only the ones that can be filled end up coming home with me. I found this particular piece in an antique shop here in New York City and fell in love with it immediately.

Before I even knew this pitcher was of British origin, it conjured up thoughts of a lovely English garden for me. The wonderful botanical vibe is inspiring, not just because of the many floral combinations it brings to mind, but because of the mood it evokes. It feels romantic and old world.

What About the Palette?

The moody palette, with its smoky gray and black touches, feels dark and sophisticated—almost sexy. An unexpected color combination like this can be a lot of fun to work with.

Who Is the Client?

This inspiration is perfect for the bride who might love floral-patterned china, but doesn't want her entire wedding to come off looking like a giant tea party. I also think it works well for a couple that's inspired by vintage tones and objects.

Where and When?

I definitely envision this event taking place outdoors, so this inspiration is ideal for summer. I can see the guests sipping lemonade in the late afternoon sun and then dancing under the stars once night falls. An old estate or mansion with sprawling lawns and gardens would make for a beautiful backdrop, as would a museum with a garden or terrace for cocktails.

My Focus

My focus is to illustrate how you can beautifully marry the slightly "granny" British notes of the pitcher with a more edgy, moody aesthetic, creating an event that feels young and interesting.

MOOD

The botanical vibe conjures up thoughts of a lovely English garden—one in which I would want to wile away as many hours as I could spare.

COLOR

I'm really drawn to the moody, yet romantic, color palette of this piece. The smoky gray and black make the magenta and green feel chic and sophisticated.

SHAPE/FORM

The graceful shape and delicate nature of the ceramic are two of my favorite qualities about this pitcher.

HUNTED AND GATHERED

OPPOSITE I let the English quality of this pitcher lead me along. The dark and moody palette is rich and inspiring.

VINTAGE TEA TIN—A lot of these old tea tins from years gone by can get pretty wacky, making them intriguing objects to work with. The exotic image on this tin is fascinating; I can't help but wonder, who was this woman?

PLUMS—The color of these small fruits is deep and lovely.

VINTAGE FABRIC FLOWERS—A direct reference to the floral motif on my pitcher, these vintage flowers are charming.

METAL LEAVES—The brassy finish on these leaves is really appealing.

COCKTAIL NAPKINS—I love the striking contrast of the black-and-white napkins together.

MOROCCAN TEA GLASSES—These are great for holding votives or small floral arrangements.

FABRIC FLOWER GARLAND—Can you imagine the wonderful parties that would have been decorated with a vintage garland like this?

VINTAGE SPOON—There is something definitively English about this silver spoon.

BLACK GLASS TROPHY CUP—I couldn't wait to create the perfect accent arrangement with this piece.

BEADED FLOWERS—These little vintage flowers are so dear and add a bit of sparkle.

RIGHT For this bouquet, I played up the painterly quality of the English pitcher. I chose 'Tropical Butterfly,' a unique variegated variety of *Dianthus*—the petals look as if someone has just daubed paint all over them. I paired them with *Veronica*, a spindly plant that looks feathery and soft. The bluish-purple clematis is a great accent to the *Dianthus*, while the passion vines add a whimsy to the whole piece. It feels organic, despite the tight construction.

OPPOSITE In a modern space, a dramatic flower arrangement like this seven-foot-tall piece feels extra special. I found this old garden urn to use as the base—the black finish has worn away in a charming way, revealing warm red tones underneath. Once I'd created a sturdy structure from mountain laurel branches, I began adding in the flowers. Toward the bottom, I tucked in two types of hydrangeas—a lacecap variety called 'Emotion' in a periwinkle tone and a more classic variety in purple. From there, I filled in the top with purple Dutch delphinium. An arrangement like this is great as a welcome piece or perhaps as an anchor to the end of an aisle.

ABOVE The black metal garden planters at the heart of this table setting feel very British and secret garden–like, which hints at our inspirational English pitcher. I planted them full of hot pink *Phalaenopsis* orchids and then nestled in some purple heart, which has this trailing vinelike foliage, to help disguise the planting. Traditionally moss is used to cover orchids and plantings of this nature, but I like how overgrown and exotic the vines feel tumbling onto the table. Arrangements like this are great for repurposing. Prior to the reception, these could have lined the aisle at your ceremony. Black-and-white-patterned napkins make all other embellishments unnecessary.

OPPOSITE Classic English tea sandwiches are the perfect little something to serve for a casual event or perhaps for brunch the day after your wedding. Tea & Sympathy in New York City put together this assortment for us. I always find my way to this lovely shop when I'm missing London and am in need of a trip across the pond. If you don't have a great little spot like this to turn to, any good deli should be willing to whip something up for you. I set the mini sandwiches on this English-looking antique silver platter and then tucked in some perfectly ripe cherries as an added treat. The mini arrangement of soft purple hydrangeas helps to make it feel more special.

LEFT I love shopping at the flower markets here in New York City—I pulled together this little hand-tied bouquet of *Nigella*, peonies, and *Gomphrena* after one such trip. I'm constantly amazed by the number of beautiful hybrids coming from countries relatively new to the flower industry, like Japan, Israel, and New Zealand. The markets are such a wonderful source of inspiration and can be an invaluable resource for you when planning your event. Visit them about a year in advance to see what will be in season for your big day. This will allow you to plan your flower budget accordingly, as things that are out of season can quickly become pricey at their off time of year.

OPPOSITE Our English pitcher translates beautifully into this space, which has romantic floral notes and a rich green garden setting. A wedding canopy like this creates a beautiful space under which to say your vows, making it a popular choice for both Jewish and non-Jewish couples alike.

Note that if you are including a canopy, it's important to build a sturdy structure that won't blow over in a slightly stiff breeze. I used a simple metal gazebo base that was easily covered with greenery to ensure that it would stay put. Once the base was in place, I wove mountain laurel branches around the structure, completely disguising it beneath a nest of branches.

I tucked delphinium flowers throughout the branches, bringing in this romantic purple hue. Dutch delphinium is a great flower that people unfortunately often overlook. You get a lot of bang for your buck, as the stems are often three- to four-feet long, with flowers blooming up the entire length. I love the way these purple delphinium pop against the magical green curtain of that old weeping willow tree.

To keep the romance trailing all the way down the aisle, I adorned each row of chairs with a small bunch of deep purple hydrangeas accented with a complementary double-faced satin ribbon. A few delphinium blossoms sprinkled in the grass finished things off nicely. I like the idea of doing just a few flowers down the aisle, rather than creating an entire carpet out of blooms; it's more modern and fresh.

ABOVE It is a nice idea to host a light brunch the day after your wedding. Everyone involved is typically tired and worn out from all the preparation and partying, so it's nice to do something a bit simple. Some beautiful English scones with lemon curd, jam, and clotted cream are a great way to send off your guests. These came from Tea & Sympathy, my favorite place to go for all things British in New York City. A lovely little spread like this could also work nicely for a daytime event.

THIS PAGE The pinky-purple color featured on our pitcher is clearly the driving force behind this bouquet—the peonies and fuzzy *Gomphrena* echo the shade perfectly. One of my favorite things about the pitcher is the black detailing, so I worked in some black-and-white *Nigella* blooms to give this bouquet that same feel.

LEFT Most people find themselves attracted to more than one design aesthetic, making it tough to narrow down what type of event they want to create. While our English pitcher has a decidedly traditional vibe to it, I show here how easily this inspiration can be transformed into a modern table setting.

The focal point of this table is the array of stellar black lacquered candlesticks from Global Table in SoHo, Manhattan. Paired with long black taper candles, the effect is striking. The black is unexpected, making these pieces feel more modern. I opted for stemless glassware, as I didn't want the profile of the glasses to interfere with the long lines of the candles.

To keep this table modern, I left off any linens. From the ceramic vessel filled with garden roses, purple clematis, and purple grapes, to the small compotes boasting dark cherries and plums around the table, it's the black that makes everything feel cohesive. The cherries and plums are a sweet alternative to small satellite flower arrangements; they look marvelous and give your guests something to nibble on between courses. A plum at each place setting was an appealing finishing touch.

WELCOME GIFTS

- Remember, some of your guests have likely traveled a long way—all of them, if you're having a destination wedding. So let them know, the minute they arrive, just how much you appreciate their making the trip.
- Welcome gifts don't have to be elaborate; small or large, your message of gratitude will be immediately felt.
- It's nice to have the gift waiting for your guests as they arrive. It's likely they already have too many things to carry—don't add one more into the mix by having your gift presented to them at the front desk. Have either your wedding planner or a member of the hotel staff drop each gift off so that it's waiting for your loved ones as soon as they enter their rooms.
- Most hotels will charge you a drop-off fee, so check with the concierge beforehand to see how they typically handle this sort of request.

RIGHT These hand-molded tea leaf and dogwood flower–shaped sugars from Arak Kanofsky Studios are charming. They're the perfect accent to sweeten up your run-of-the-mill coffee-and-tea service.

OPPOSITE This thoughtful welcome gift, filled with everything one needs to enjoy the perfect cup of tea, is a lovely representation of our English pitcher inspiration. Gifts for the Good Life designed this array to be enjoyed either right away or upon returning home after the wedding festivities.

What you'll find inside: This white tray, with its decoupage floral design, makes it easy for your guests to take their tea-inspired picnic to go. On the tray they'll find inscribed the lyrics from Cole Porter's famous ballad "Night and Day," an extra touch to garner an extra smile. Consider using a few lines from your wedding song to personalize the piece. The printed tea towel echoes the sentiments of the gift, with a warm and lasting "Welcome." To start their day off right, your guests will find Good Morning Tea, a loose English breakfast variety, presented in a lavender jute sack. Atop that dear little picnic basket is delicious artisanal fig-and-black-tea jam, waiting to be enjoyed with a few slices of mini toast. There are tea strainers, honey sticks, and floral shaped sugar cubes to ensure they'll have everything they need. A few indulgent English biscuits are included too. And what better way to end the evening than with a relaxing cup of 1,000 Nights of Passion tea, a Good Night variety also found inside one of those lovely lavender jute sacks.

OPPOSITE   While the shape of this garden bouquet is rather classical, the textures help to make it a bit wilder and less predictable. The yummy raspberry-colored roses pop against the more muted greens of the *Scabiosa* pods and blooming oregano, while the creamy lacecap hydrangeas add a nice touch of softness. I love the way this light pink smooth cotton ribbon looks with the brighter roses. Remember that tones of the same color don't have to match exactly to complement one another.

ABOVE   A stunning menu like this one from Arak Kanofsky Studios is so decorative and intriguing that it completely negates the need for any further adornment at each place setting. Its glamorous fan shape and vintage golden tassel are a delicate interpretation of the old-world influence of our English pitcher.

ABOVE Inspired by the formal and fragile nature of the English pitcher, Gifts for the Good Life crafted these lovely crystal paperweights as another keepsake option for our pitcher-inspired event. The word "Love" scripted inside expresses the ultimate sentiment of the day.

OPPOSITE This accent arrangement has a decadent, dreamy, almost Alice-in-Wonderland quality. I gathered English garden roses right from the grounds and then worked with smaller spray roses, lavender, sweet pea, green clematis leaves, and these unique grayish-purple ferns to fill out the display.

RIGHT, OPPOSITE I created this whole table to take on a fancy-meets-rustic feeling, where the two worlds come together seamlessly in one contained setting. Our elegant pitcher feels like a marriage of both beautiful things, with its delicate shape and wild garden motif.

I started with this chic gray linen tablecloth that has a lovely, smooth texture. The cloth worked perfectly with these rustic wooden chairs I found at a flea market. The ornate silver flatware and the platinum-edged plates gave me that fancy touch I was craving. These etched vintage water glasses are elegant; their unique shape and delicate detailing make them a lovely addition to this setting. While I stuck with one style, consider sourcing several different vintage glasses and mixing them up on your table.

This abundant flower arrangement, filled with lacecap hydrangeas, *Brodiaea*, fluttery sweet pea, and jasmine vine, is one of my genuine favorites; it feels so happy and romantic. The dark negative space between the flowers is refreshing—it's nice when flowers have a little room to breathe. The small blue floral pattern on the white footed bowl is a lovely nod to our inspirational pitcher, with its dainty botanical motif.

My favorite detail here is the sweet *Brodiaea* flower wrapped around the crisp white napkin; I love how it elegantly brings the centerpiece down into each place setting. Make sure you work with a plant with a long, flexible stem, as you want to be able to tie the stem to itself. It's a nice play on the more traditional ribbon-tied napkin.

OPPOSITE The rich purple tones in this loosely fashioned bouquet are exquisite. I used tree peonies—a more delicate variety that grows in an array of interesting colors, fluttery sweet pea, and star-shaped *Brodiaea* to create this slightly Bohemian-feeling nosegay.

ABOVE Our inspirational English pitcher has a delightful painterly quality to it, so I thought it might be fun to play that up in a very literal way. Taking direction from the floral motif on the pitcher, Arak Kanofsky Studios and I created these playful mini painted canvases masquerading as escort cards.

ABOVE Here the floral pattern adorning our inspirational pitcher was meticulously replicated on top of each white chocolate–covered, jam-filled cake, a deliciously literal interpretation of our pitcher. These cakes show how even an intricate pattern can translate into a wide variety of accessories.

OPPOSITE This petite arrangement is all about playing up the chic black glass trophy. I wanted the flowers to complement the vessel, rather than the other way around. I paired this deep plum red *Scabiosa* with some fragrant purple basil to create this intense, moody little moment.

SEASHELLS

Why Seashells?

I cherish my childhood memories of collecting seashells with my dad. We would spend hours combing the beach in search of that perfect shell to bring home for my mom. Come summertime, it's just what we always did. Now as an adult, I still love to spend hours walking along the edge of the sea, my bare feet in the water, hunting for just one more special shell before heading in for the night. I feature shells in this book because I think everyone has an affinity for collecting them. A seashell is often the only lasting memento from a family beach vacation, eventually taking up residence on a bookshelf or among its fellows in an old jar, to be admired for years to come.

Sentimentality aside, a grouping of seashells can be tremendously inspiring. Their delicate shapes and fragile nature can conjure up a wealth of ideas. They're useful for creating an entire mood as well—consider the sights and sounds of a seaside town and draw on all of that as inspiration, not just the shells themselves. Don't forget about all the other sea-dwelling creatures that might evoke an idea or two—corals and kelp can be beautiful. Let the sea inspire your menu, with a delicious fish course or a fun and modern take on the raw bar. And think about the types of plants and flowers that are found by the water—they're often much more interesting than your normal garden-variety rose.

What About the Palette?

For this inspiration, I have kept the earthy colors mostly muted and quiet, though I often give them a very crisp and contemporary twist. The overriding cream and gray tones, paired with these rich brown and soft pink accents, come together beautifully to create a chic and modern palette that I adore.

Who Is the Client?

Obviously, a couple that loves the romance of the beach and sea is going to be attracted to an inspirational choice like seashells. This inspiration is also perfect for someone who is looking for a fresh approach to a more earthy color palette.

Where and When?

These design ideas would be lovely at a seaside wedding, but they can look beautiful anywhere, from your backyard to an urban loft space. I would say spring and summer are the best seasons for this look if you go in a more literal direction, but keep in mind that if your driving inspiration is simply palette-based, these colors could be stunning in the fall.

My Focus

I find that many of my clients love design ideas stirred up by earthy, coastal locations, yet they struggle with how to balance those ideas with a more urban aesthetic, so that is my focus with this chapter. My idea here is not to plaster shells onto everything that will sit still long enough, but instead to illustrate many subtle variations on this theme.

MOOD
There are few things that compare to watching the sunset from the beach, feeling the sand cool down between your toes. I really wanted to tap into that experience throughout the following pages.

COLOR
I love the quiet, earthy colors found in these seashells. The cream, gray, rich brown, and muted pink come together to create a chic and modern palette.

SHAPE/FORM
It's so easy to get inspired by the numerous shapes and patterns that wash up on the shore. I never tire of their beauty.

HUNTED AND GATHERED

OPPOSITE I have collected here objects that felt a bit weathered to me, as if they'd spent a good deal of time tumbling around in the surf before being rescued. The color palette is of course important as well, as are the shapes and myriad of textures.

PINK VASE—I love the shell-like shape of this little vase. The coral-pink color relates perfectly to the inspirational shells that I found.

GRAY MUG—This I chose for its gray outer hue, which is an important color in this palette. This brownish gray is one of those distinct, in-between earthy tones you see often in the seashell world.

DRIFTWOOD CARVING—I can just imagine this piece, covered in barnacles, at the bottom of the ocean, a castoff from some sunken ship.

FLORAL PITCHER—The lovely bone color of this pitcher mimics the base tone of a lot of shells. The browns and pinks featured in the floral design pick up on the same wonderful shades present in our inspirational shells.

RIBBONS—In our elegant seashell palette.

SILVER FABRIC—You know how the sea takes on that silver, shimmery tone as the sun sinks down behind the ocean for the night? This fabric instantly made me think of that magical time of day.

FABRIC NETTING—This fancy netting felt like couture fishing gear—I adore it!

RUSTY COPPER VESSEL—This old jelly mold, with its unique rustiness, made me think of some wacky sea creature, or perhaps something one might find when diving for sunken treasure.

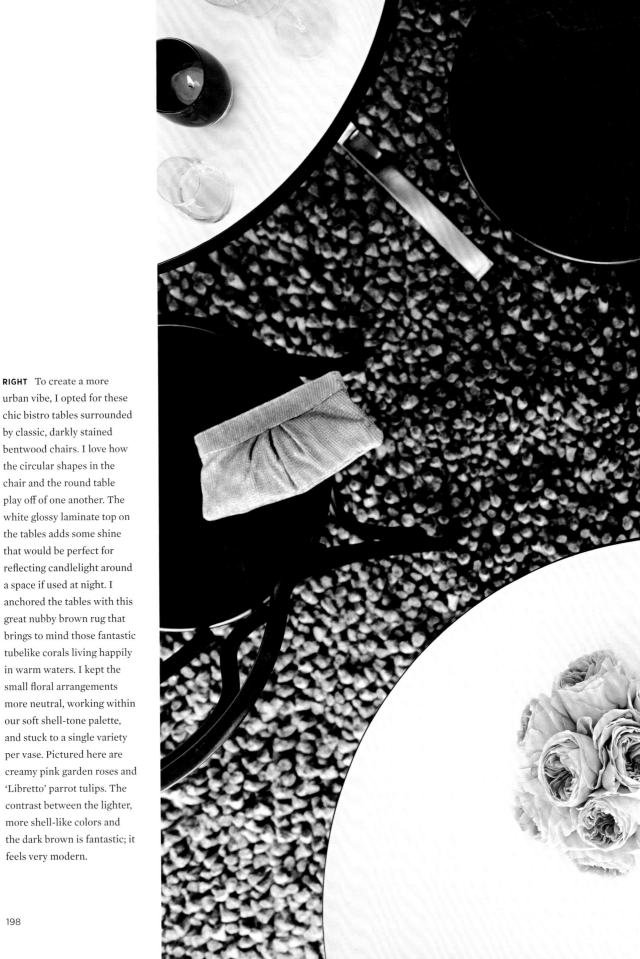

RIGHT To create a more urban vibe, I opted for these chic bistro tables surrounded by classic, darkly stained bentwood chairs. I love how the circular shapes in the chair and the round table play off of one another. The white glossy laminate top on the tables adds some shine that would be perfect for reflecting candlelight around a space if used at night. I anchored the tables with this great nubby brown rug that brings to mind those fantastic tubelike corals living happily in warm waters. I kept the small floral arrangements more neutral, working within our soft shell-tone palette, and stuck to a single variety per vase. Pictured here are creamy pink garden roses and 'Libretto' parrot tulips. The contrast between the lighter, more shell-like colors and the dark brown is fantastic; it feels very modern.

ABOVE, OPPOSITE I rented some clear Plexiglas ghost chairs so that the wonderful lines of this table wouldn't disappear behind a mob of dark chairs. The reflective creamy white surface of the table is lovely and shell-like; it couldn't have been more perfect for dinner at our shell-inspired event. I set the table with creamy milk glass plates, topped them with crisp white linen napkins, and then placed a big beautiful white clamshell on top of each. To keep things simple, I worked peonies, garden roses, and blushy pink lilacs into three identical arrangements. The square glass vases were perfect for adding in a rustic, yet modern, touch.

THOUGHTS ON FURNITURE RENTALS

- People tend to think flowers are the only way to define the look of an event, but furniture can have just as much, if not more, of an impact on the overall ambiance. Your rental choices will dictate the look and feel of your wedding, so make sure they are a big part of your planning. You can order a slew of stunning centerpieces, but if each one is sitting on an unattractive table, the effect is totally lost.

- Rental companies are offering more and more unique options these days, so explore all there is to choose from before making any final decisions.

- In lieu of the classic linen-covered rounds, consider renting some chic and modern bistro tables for your cocktail hour.

- Even if you don't have the budget to rent tons of furniture, it can be great to do a few key vignettes that sort of set the space off in a new and more interesting way. Sometimes clients think they need to rent hundreds of pieces of furniture, but you can create a few nooks around the dance floor that give the space a bit of a more luxurious feel.

  P.S. If you're not going to do a lot of furniture, make sure you choose pieces that have a lot of character and that make a significant statement in small numbers

- Ghost chairs, made of clear Plexiglas, add a dreamy, light quality to any table. They allow the lines of the furniture to show through, making them perfect for any unique table that can go linenless. Very often the number of chairs can overpower a space—ghost chairs obviously eliminate this concern, as they hardly show up at all.

- Think of the furniture as a great prop for photographs. A photo of, say, your great-aunt Dorothy is much more interesting and lively if she is seated in a luxurious velvet chair as opposed to one of her taking a break on a plastic folding rental. The décor is about creating moments that you will remember for a lifetime, so use pieces that inspire you and make you smile.

- Consider renting proper garden furniture for an outdoor wedding, or items that look and feel like they would actually live outdoors. I'm always slightly aggravated by tables with linens out on a lawn; the tablecloths tend to look messy when blowing around, and they seem to get in the way.

SOFAS

- A few rented sofas are a nice touch; they immediately create a place of comfort and rest for your guests, letting them know where they can kick off their shoes and curl up their legs (if, of course, their wardrobe allows!).

- Use sofas to form a conversation area in your cocktail space, and for lounging at the after party.

- Sofas are perfect for elderly guests who might be better served by a comfy place to enjoy your nuptials.
- Sofas will also quickly become a central location for taking pictures, so keep that in mind when choosing one.
- Don't shy away from using them outside. While it might seem strange at first, upholstered furniture in the great outdoors creates a wonderful juxtaposition that can work beautifully.

BENCHES

- Upholstered benches are great modern seating for your ceremony or event, but are best used when your vows are going to be brief.
- Benches help create a cleaner look, as visually your eye can move across a space unencumbered by the backs of one hundred plus chairs.
- Benches are very easy to rent.
- Benches add a nice masculine feel to a space.

TOP You cannot have a wedding without a champagne toast! I definitely recommend splurging on good champagne; the toast is a moment when your guests will be focused on just that one thing, so treat them to something they will enjoy. What better to serve at our shell-infused party than pink champagne? I love this Veuve Clicquot—the color is a perfect coral shade. In an effort to keep things interesting and modern, I mixed up the flute shapes. I draped a single calla lily on the tray as an elegant accent.

RIGHT While I adore working with flowers, sometimes the effect a single variety of foliage can have is really special. Here, I filled these vintage pewter vases with dusty miller and a feathery foliage I found in the flower markets. The soft texture of the dusty miller is quite inviting, while the foliage reminds me of something that might happily grow in a tropical reef. I anchored them together with gold metallic netting.

OPPOSITE These little Saarinen tables are amazing; they're distinct design pieces that will have a big impact on your décor. They're easy to rent and perfect for your cocktail hour or lounge area after the reception. I placed this sweet arrangement of dusty miller, eucalyptus, and white garden roses in a white compote on top to make the cool marble seem more inviting.

Menu

Appetizer
Maryland Crab Cake with Charred Corn, Jicama and a
Roasted Red Pepper Aioli

Salad

Entrees
Grilled Filet Migon with Oven Roasted Tomatoes
in a Port Wine Sauce
Hazelnut Encrusted Rack of Lamb with Mint Apple Compote
Pan Seared Halibut with Merlot Demi Glace

Accompaniments
Truffle Potato Pot Pie
Julienne Squash, Zucchini & Carrots

Dessert
Chocolate Tulip filled with Orange Sorbet & Fresh Berries

ABOVE The slightly off shape of this gorgeous plate reminds me of the irregularity of shells, making it a perfect choice for setting our table. I also adore the pinky-gold rim—it's just like the inside edge of a pried-open oyster shell. It feels special and delicate. I chose an open-weave linen napkin to add texture to the setting and then wrapped a lovely golden silk ribbon around the menu and napkin itself, creating a nice little package for the lucky diner. A sprig of eucalyptus finishes off the setting.

THIS PAGE I didn't want to neglect some of the more intense oranges, ambers, and browns that can be found as well. In that spirit, I rented some burnt orange wingback chairs and paired them up with these modern creamy taupe banquets to create a special little seating area.

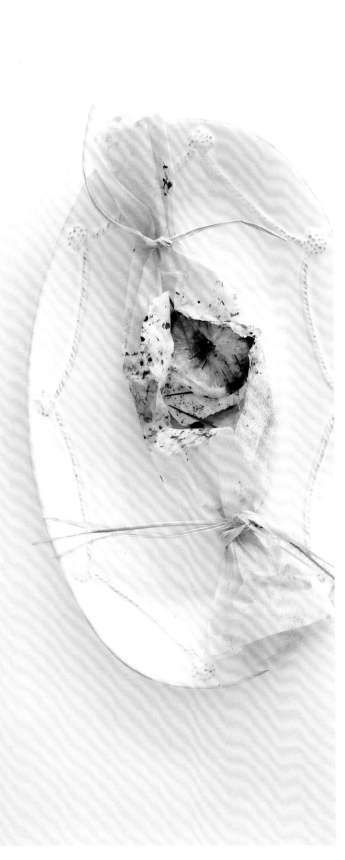

- Don't forget to pick everything up and look at what's happening underneath. The bottom surface of a plate or tray may be just as lovely as the top and, when used as the main surface, will give your food some height.
- Don't forget to inquire about any and all serving pieces that will be used at your catered event. Ask to see the different types of trays your caterer has to offer and then consider bringing separate rentals or even purchased pieces into the mix.
- Using vintage trays is one of my favorite ways to display food; they make everything feel more special and exotic. Check local flea markets and antique shops to find a nice mix of pieces. Ask family members to show any lovely old items they may have to offer as well.

LEFT The meal served at your reception will have just as much of an impact on your guests as the way the venue is decorated, so remember that while the food should taste delicious, it should also have visual appeal. I worked with my friends at Marcey Brownstein Catering & Events to create this beautiful dish. Serving fish cooked in parchment, elegantly known as *poisson en papillote*, is a more chic reference to our inspiration than, say, handing your guests a plate of mussels and clams. I love how the presentation feels so giftlike. Inside you'll find halibut, cooked simply with just lemon and chives. The decoration on this Juliska plate made me think of ropes strewn around a beautiful old ship. Serving a lovely, simple meal on an interesting plate elevates the entire presentation.

OPPOSITE This *poisson en papillote* is a more rustic version of the former. Our idea was to serve this version to your gentlemen guests, while the ladies would receive the previous, more-refined version. The shell shape of the parchment package couldn't be more spot-on—when it bakes, the paper browns around the edges in a wonderful irregular pattern, instantly adding to the shell-like appearance. Inside, guests will find a beautifully rustic meal of halibut baked with tomatoes, capers, chives, and lemon. I adore this glazed Astier de Villatte plate with the shell-like beading around the edge. It's nice to serve a simple dish on a beautiful plate. And the rustic dark wooden table underneath is amazing; the contrast is startling in such a lovely way.

THOUGHTS ON CREATING A MODERN RAW BAR

- Use the soft shell palette to shape your food choices.
- Serve food inside of a shell, either its own or another's. It incorporates the inspirational object in a sophisticated way.
- Use white trays, like the rustic glazed ones pictured, to set off the colors nicely.
- Make sure to serve things like ceviche in small individual glass cups or bowls. The glass allows the food to be part of the décor, while the small serving makes it easier to eat. You could even consider using small glass votives (which you can easily purchase by the dozens at any craft store) if you find some you really love, but be sure to check that they are made to be food-safe.
- Use different colored sea salts to give the illusion that food is sitting in sand. Remember, however, that the food shouldn't sit directly in the salt, but rather rest on top inside its serving piece.

OPPOSITE, LEFT   I thought it would be fun to have a raw bar at our seashell-inspired event. This idea is modern, and with a really chic and interesting presentation, the raw bar could easily become the main focus of your cocktail hour or reception. Instead of just tossing out some trays, I overturned these large stone vases and used them as platforms with which to elevate the food. Even though our focus is a more modern display, it's important to maintain an earthy touch with an inspiration like shells. These stone vessels are perfect—their clean shape is modern, but the stone keeps them earthy. The glazed white trays set off the color of the food nicely. Marcey Brownstein Catering & Events created a tempting menu: bay scallop ceviche with watermelon relish and a tortilla swizzle; poached shrimp and citrus salad; chili chive tuna tartare on a potato gaufrette perched on a scallop shell.

THIS PAGE While most people tend to believe a bouquet should be held toward the front of your body, I think a version that can be cradled like this is absolutely lovely. I layered wild grasses, exotic ginger, *Amaranthus*, and lotus flowers loosely on top of one another to create this effortless look.

THIS PAGE These white-washed tables and chairs are ideal for a seaside or garden wedding. Imagine how lovely dozens of them would look scattered across a sweeping green lawn, or artfully arranged on the beach. This is the perfect example of how to let furniture define the mood.

RIGHT This centerpiece focuses on form rather than the flowers. My goal was to create a coral reef down the center of this rectangular table and, in doing so, end up with an amazingly alive sculptural runner. I used resin coral and a variety of real shells as the base and then tucked in numerous textural grasses and *Scabiosa* pods to mimic those wonderful little sea creatures that might call my reef home. This version of the seashell palette, incorporating the gold, yellow, brown, and gray, feels sophisticated and chic. I love the airiness these chairs and clean white table lend to the whole setting.

To let the reef really be the star here, I kept each place setting minimal; from the plate to the napkin, to the pure white sand dollars resting on top, nothing else could steal the show.

LEFT, ABOVE When I found these paper shells and fish I knew I had to use them. I definitely didn't want to incorporate too many real shells, as I think the literalness of it would detract from using an object as your inspiration rather than your theme. That's why the paper shells are perfect; they obviously look just like shells, but there's a playfulness there that wouldn't have been otherwise. Every boutonniere is unique, allowing each honored gentleman to feel special. I used different combinations of eucalyptus, jasmine, dusty miller, and wax flower, and then accented each with some grosgrain ribbon.

OPPOSITE Using seashells as your muse doesn't mean the inspiration has to stop there. Think outside the box and use the whole sea as a place to draw from. For example, this wooden table appears to be made from a giant piece of driftwood that could have washed ashore on some rocky beach in New England. The wide variety of small glass bottles dotted down the center of the table creates a nontraditional runner that's a fun nod to the old message-in-a-bottle idea without being tacky. They also remind me of collecting sea glass when I was a child. I layered some of the bottles on top of this great milk glass tray to add in a reflective surface that can highlight the milky votives twinkling well into the evening. I used anemones, garden roses, sweet pea, *Ranunculus*, wax flower, dusty miller foliage, and eucalyptus.

OPPOSITE Foliage is great for creating swags, like this one featuring wax flowers and jasmine, as it generally holds up better for longer periods of time. Flowers, once cut, will wilt quickly, especially in the heat of the day. I prefer a garland to feel a bit wild, rather than structured; the looseness makes it more forgiving and interesting. I accented the swag with these rosy pink ribbons, once again pulling from the many lovely colors shells have to offer.

I love this white-washed wooden chair and table for a more modern take on the cocktail hour. If you're having an outdoor wedding, think about garden furniture—either rentals or your own. For a more intimate affair, consider asking your friends and family about borrowing their outdoor furniture. You might find that a fun mixture of what everyone has to offer is the perfect solution.

ABOVE I created this softly cascading bouquet by working with hellebores and white sweet pea flowers. The hellebores are definitely the star of this show, but the sweet pea adds a delicate layer that complements them perfectly. I tucked this unique foliage in for its fluttery, almost sea creature–like quality.

LEFT This sweet little loosely tied bouquet reminds me of an Italian bridesmaid waiting patiently for the festivities to begin. I mixed freesia, peonies, *Ranunculus*, and wax flowers, all in creamy tones, and then pulled a colored ribbon from the richer tones in our palette. I love how alive this nosegay feels.

OPPOSITE Here I created an aisle and altar clearly inspired by our gorgeous shells, but fit for a modern urban environment. The whole vibe is simple and very unfussy, almost Zen-like.

I chose nontraditional white upholstered benches to give the space a modern feel. They're great for a shorter ceremony, where the guests will be seated for only a brief time. The white linen fabric and crisp dark wooden legs are clean looking; they have a nice beachy vibe too. Then, to soften the wall and add warmth to the space, I hung some creamy muslin as a backdrop.

I accented each seating aisle with glass hurricane lanterns that were filled with tiny shells to anchor the glittery golden ivory pillar candles placed inside. You could easily use sand or rocks instead, but I couldn't resist this opportunity to introduce our inspiration in a sweet way. Don't forget how versatile glass hurricanes can be. They are very easy to repurpose at your cocktail hour and reception alike. You can line a walkway with them, place a few on your seating-card table, and accent any number of entrances or little nooks with glowing light. Repurposing pieces is a great way to keep the budget down.

The magnolia branches at the end of the aisle really are the stars of this show. The beautiful pinky-purple flowers blossoming from the branches have a wonderful sea-like quality that makes me think of some little shelled creature living among the coral. They instantly draw the eye and let guests know just where your special moment will take place. Depending on how far apart you place them, and how high they extend, the branches can naturally create an arch perfect for saying your vows beneath.

Supporting the magnolia branches are these wonderful, slightly rustic-looking white metal urns. I love how they look as if they've been tumbled around in the surf a bit, revealing the metal surface beneath. And finally, giving glamorous height to our arrangements, are these two gorgeous wooden pillars. They're a nice urban take on seafaring driftwood.

ACKNOWLEDGMENTS

Holly Ash Greenwald, thank you for your undying loyalty, and for bringing laughter, lightness, and joy into my life.

Yfat Reiss Gendell, you are truly amazing. I love your energy and passion. Thank you for believing in my work. I now understand that having an incredible agent is essential. Thank you to everyone at Foundry Literary + Media, including Stephanie Abou, Hannah Brown Gordon, and Cecilia Campbell-Weslind, for all your hard work and commitment to this project.

Martha, your generous support of my work put me right here and made this book possible. You, your work, and your team are forever a part of my journey, and I'm so grateful for the many invaluable experiences.

Rebecca Thuss and Patrick Farrell, thank you for all your meticulous work and your commitment to making the most beautiful book. Your passion for design is something I cherish and admire.

Thank you to an awesome team at Matthew Robbins Design: Kimmy, Thu, Teresa, Nico, Catherine, Melissa, Jo, and Amanda—you all worked so very hard to make every shoot a success.

Thank you to everyone at Stewart, Tabori & Chang: Jennifer Levesque, editor (for loving the project from the start); Ivy McFadden, managing editor; Leslie Stoker, publisher; Ankur Ghosh, production manager; Thuss+Farrell, designer; Michelle Ishay-Cohen, art director; Claire Bamundo, publicity; Kerry Leibling, marketing; and Wesley Royce, assistant editor.

Marcia Ceppos, thank you for the years of inspiration!

Rosemary Warren, thank you for being there when I was new to New York City and relying heavily on the kindness of friends.

Maria Vella, you were the most exquisite mentor, and I thank my lucky stars every day for stumbling into your magical world. Zolita Vella, thank you for your incredible eye. Your amazing finds fill the pages of this book and were an invaluable piece of the initial inspiration.

Darcy Miller and the *Martha Stewart Weddings* team, thank you for allowing me to be a part of your family for ten years. I'm proud to finally have a book to share with you all.

Kathryn Thuss, your patience and ability to listen were two very special qualities I desperately needed during this process. Thank you for the fantastic work.

Thank you to all of my fabulous friends and colleagues who supplied their products and services to many of the chapters in this book—you know who you are!

Mom and Dad, thank you for always supporting my creative endeavors. Grandma, thank you for a lifetime of inspiration and encouragement.

Last but certainly not least, thank you to all of the incredible clients who have allowed me to be a part of their beautiful weddings and fantastic celebrations over the years.

RESOURCES

Paper Goods
Arak Kanofsky Studios
www.arakkanofskystudios.com

Modern Press
www.modern-letterpress.com

Calligraphy
Nancy Howell
www.nancyhowell.com

Catering
Marcey Brownstein Catering
www.marceybrownstein.com

Desserts & Sweet Treats
One Girl Cookies
www.onegirlcookies.com

Sugar Sweet Sunshine
www.sugarsweetsunshine.com

GoGo Pops
www.go-gopops.com

Ceci Cela
www.cecicelanyc.com

Bridesmaids Dresses
Simple Silhouettes
www.simpledress.com

Nieves Lavi
www.nieveslavi.com

Ribbons & Trimmings
Tinsel Trading
www.tinseltrading.com

Mokuba
www.mokubany.com

May Arts
www.mayarts.com

Bell'occhio
www.bellocchio.com

Tabletop & Accessories
ABC Home
www.abchome.com

Global Table
www.globaltable.com

Glassybaby
www.glassybaby.com

Fabric
Tinsel Trading
www.tinseltrading.com

Grayline Linen
www.graylinelinen.com

B&J Fabrics
www.bandjfabrics.com

Rental Equipment & Furniture
Party Rental LTD
www.partyrentalltd.com

Greenroom
www.yourgreenroom.com

Surfaces & Backdrops
Deborah Freedman
www.deborahfreedman.com

Surface Studio
www.surfacestudio.com

Graham & Brown
www.grahambrown.com

Venues
632 Hudson
www.632onhudson.com

Locusts-on-Hudson
www.locustsonhudson.com

Buttermilk Falls Inn
www.buttermilkfallsinn.com

Ramscale Studios
www.ramscale.com

INDEX